As individuals, we can each make an effort to reconnect ourselves to the Earth. We must rediscover what we have lost, and in order for it to have any real value, it must be a personal discovery.

Cultivating a closer relationship with Mother Earth is entirely subjective. Some may choose to spend more time out-of-doors. Some may choose to join or even organize a group that focuses upon some specific or general environmental issue. Some may educate others. All of us must become living examples of our ability to change.

We can work on creating and developing a relationship with Earth, just as we would a human friend. By learning how to "read" the Earth, to detect her energy spots and use the energy of those sacred places as the Ancients did, we can awaken our intuition for greater planetary awareness and better self-awareness as well.

From the Introduction

TERRAVISION

*A Traveler's Guide
to the Living Planet Earth*

Page Bryant

BALLANTINE BOOKS • NEW YORK

DEDICATION

To the living Earth

and

the Native American peoples

who have taught us to walk in beauty.

Library of Congress Catalog Card Number: 90-93463

ISBN 0-345-35835-X

Manufactured in the United States of America

First Edition: March 1991

THE EARTH

I am the Earth
I am the great terrestrial mother.
My body was born from fires of Apollo.
My oceans gave birth to infant life.
My mountains rise up to meet the sky
In grateful praise.
My valleys shelter my children.
I am the Earth.
I am Fertile, for I am filled with
New breath from the Sun each day.
I am the Earth.
Precious gemstones are my bones.
Minerals of many varieties shape
My ever-changing body.
Plants come forth from my soil.
Animals walk upon my body in
Their dance of life.
All my precious children dance together
In praise of life—I am Earth.

Albion

CONTENTS

PREFACE

We've seen the cherry blossoms,
We've viewed the harvest moon.
Who dare to say this life
Is not worth living after all?

KUMAGAI NAOYOSHI

I look outside the window of my home in Sedona, Arizona, and gaze upon some of the most beautiful land on Mother Earth. I see shapes formed aeons ago by wind and water, standing silent, ancient red rock sentinels over the high desert landscape. There was a time when I felt that Sedona was the most sacred place on the planet. But through my studies and personal experiences with the Earth and her energies, I have come to know that all land is sacred.

If we stop to ponder how vast our universe truly is, we can understand why our tiny blue planet seems insignificant amidst it all. With as much as we know about the Cosmos, we still don't know if our planet is unique or just one among possibly millions of life-bearing bodies sprinkled throughout space. We don't have a single shred of evidence to prove or disprove that there is life on any other planet. Are we unique? Astronomical statistics say that's unlikely. For example, if we limit our speculation to the existence of *intelligent* life, and restrict our search to the *Milky Way Galaxy*, we find that we are dealing with approximately two hundred billion stars. Not all stars are like our sun. Some are smaller, some far bigger, while others are members of double or multiple star systems. If we leave out all other suns and consider only those similar to our star in luminosity, we are left with approximately 5 percent of all stars in the galaxy that *may* have planets swirling around them. I once read an account that dwindled it down to 1 percent, but that would still leave over two billion solar systems in our galaxy that may have life-bearing planets like the Earth. In short: There could be life-forms in our general region of the galaxy, but we do not *know* this to be true, leaving our perspective of the universe narrow, to say the least. This makes our planet special and, perhaps, unique. We may very well be living, alone, on a virtual paradise.

I have heard it said that travel is the best education one can get. In my life I have traveled to many corners of our planet Earth. Each place has a voice of its own. Experiencing the different cultures, tasting the various foods, feeling the pulse of the climates, is all wonderful and exciting. But the most educational and enriching experiences I have had can be found within the colors and fragrances of the mountains, oceans, islands, trees, and sands of the body of the Mother. I have felt the warm summer rains in Florida. I have watched the pink, round Sun sink slowly beneath the blue waters off Key West. I have seen the mist caress the green swells of the Blue Ridge and Smoky Mountains. I have smelled the sweetness of burning fields in England in the autumn, and listened to the winds of the Cornwall coast howl the secrets of the ancient past. I have stood at the feet of the Great Pyramid and stared into the silent eyes of the Sphinx. I have waded in the oceans, Atlantic and Pacific, and watched a sunset blaze above the water of the River Nile. I have seen the blue, ice-glazed summit of Denali and put down an offering to Pele's fire. I have scattered cornmeal on the rim of the Grand Canyon, and sat quietly in prayer on the bank of the river in Nebraska where the Pawnee once came to do ceremony in honor of the Great Spirit. And yet I have seen and felt so little of what there is of the Earth. I know there are peaceful valleys and great peaks I have not seen, hot desert sands I have not touched, and gentle rivers by which I have not rested. Perhaps you have not yet had the opportunity either. And perhaps that opportunity will be lost to our children. This is why the future of our Earth is so important. This is why I feel we must all do our part in assuring that the future will be.

Predictions from scientists and psychics alike tell us our future is threatened. Evidence mounts that tells a tale of waste and plundering of the planet's resources. Ominous forecasts of nuclear winter sober our minds. Statistics coldly predict that pollution, acid rain, and industrial wastes are turning the Earth into a diseased orb. The law of the Native American Seneca and Iroquois people that speaks of our responsibility to leave the Earth in a good state for seven future generations has fallen on the seemingly deaf ears of those motivated by greed and bottom-line technological progress. We have gotten out of step with the planet's natural rhythms. Artificial light blocks out the stars, hiding the presence of the celestial sphere as a part of our environment. Few of us talk to Nature anymore.

Through the years of my studies of and experiences with ecology and sacred geology, I have gone back and forth between feelings of despair and of thinking that man has gone too far in his rape of Mother Earth, to knowing, intuitively, that there is always hope. I have opted to rely on hope.

Much of my learning about the Earth and the mysteries of life itself have come as a result of a disincarnate Spirit Teacher for whom I have been the channel for some eighteen years. Albion has made few claims to his wisdom. Rather, his tactic is to present verbal statements and comments flavored with his own unique perspectives and allow those who hear them to decide if they are valid and how they might best be used for the betterment of ourselves and our planet. It was Albion who led me into a study of and an appreciation for the Earth. And it is Albion who has given me and many others a way to interpret Nature's language. Much of the information in *TerraVision*, as well as my previous books, is based upon Albion's teachings and view of Reality.

INTRODUCTION

by Sun Bear

At this time in the history of the planet, it is critical for *all* people to learn how to walk in good balance on the Earth Mother. From my travels throughout the world, I know there are many good people who want to learn to live this way, but they don't know how. TERRAVISION is going to help them find their way.

For many thousands of years my people lived upon this continent, this Turtle Island, in a way that showed great respect and love for their planetary home. The same was true for Native people all around the world. They knew how important it was to respect the circle of life—the sacred circle. They know that what happened to any part of the circle affected them, and all generations to come. When the earth was healthy, the people were healthy too. When any part of the circle became diseased, it affected everything else on the planet. Native people understood what scientists are just now beginning to discover: the earth is *alive*.

Over the earth there are many sacred places. One may be on top of a tall mountain; another along a lake shore. Many of these places were sacred to all Native people. Others were sacred to a particular tribe, family, or individual. Whenever I come to such a place or power, I make a prayer and offer tobacco because these are places where special spirits dwell—places where the heartbeat of the earth beats loudly and gives out particularly strong energy.

Native people knew how important it was to honor such places. Some tribes did this by holding sacred ceremonies, while other tribes made special pilgrimages to such places. Individuals on journeys would always stop at sacred places to make prayers and offerings and listen to the voice of the Earth.

Today, during this time of the intense earth changes, it is even more important for people to learn how to recognize and honor the Earth's sacred places. Many people tell me they would do so gladly, but they don't know *where the sites are, how to find them, and what they should do to show their respect for them.*

Page Bryant, one of my first apprentices, is a woman who knows, loves and understands the Earth and its sacredness. She has an impressive knowledge of the environment, Native peoples, and comparative religions of the Earth, and most importantly, she is a sincere seeker of spiritual truth wherever it may be found. In Page's work as a teacher, writer and psychic, she has always shown great respect for the power of the Earth and has stressed the importance of taking personal responsibility for our beautiful planet.

In the EARTH CHANGES SURVIVAL HANDBOOK, Page cautioned people about the harm now being done to the Earth. In TERRAVISION she gives us all some positive steps we can take both to heal the damage already done and to help avert future catastrophes. May this book help you find new ways to heal yourself, help the planet, and truly live in balance with the Earth.

Sun Bear
March, 1991

ACKNOWLEDGMENTS

No book comes together without the combined efforts of many people. This one is no exception. There are many individuals I must thank, for they gave of their time, knowledge, and support for the principles presented here. I must begin with my friend and secretary, Helaine McLain, who often went past the call of duty to type and assist in the many hours of research, as well as sketching the map illustrations. I am also deeply indebted to my friend and literary agent, Wabun Wind, whose faith in me and my work brought this book into reality. My thanks to my editor, Cheryl Woodruff, who believed I had something to say and helped me say it in a better way because of her expertise and her sensitivity and concern for Mother Earth. Much grateful appreciation must also go to Tek Nickerson, Sun Bear, Grandmother Twylah Nitche, Harley Swiftdeer, Fred Spinks, Karen Burt, Betsy Brown, Tom Workman, Joy and Jason Kuhn, Sharberi, Flo Calhoun, Pua and Herb Brentlinger, Lama Karma Rinchen, Jaine Smith, and William Geiss. Special thanks and love must go to my best friend and husband, Scott Guynup, for being my untiring supporter and best critic.

PART I

THE BREATH
OF
GAIA

ENDANGERED SPECIES

Dust devils swirl and gather
tumbleweeds, whisper and moan
throughout burned over forests

Cracked and gaping fields lie open
to whirlwinds of despair—no water
for the corn, nor waterways for egrets
and no milk for the cheeta's cub.

Why, why, on every hand the cry
what have we done, why are we allowed
desecration of a masterpiece?

Could it be the One decrees
fall of the lordly redwood
for a grander tree?

The same Who patiently allowed
primeval man to give way
to a Michaelangelo?

Must oceans of the planet shrink
necessitating smaller whales
allowing space for man
in greater numbers?

So speaks the head, but oh the heart
cries out for maintenance intact
of ordinary miracles—

Magnificent and hoary trees
crags and colors of Grand Canyon
pungent air and streams to marvel in
snow-covered soaring mountains
and the tender grass, cardinals
and rabbits—a million million
wonders—just for seeing—

Whatever gods are listening
do we need
a grander tree, a smaller whale?

Karen Burt

CHAPTER ONE

GAIA:
Our Beautiful Troubled Planet Earth

We sang songs that carried in their melodies
all the sounds of nature—
the running of waters, the
sighing of winds, and the calls of
the animals.
Teach these to your children,
that they may come to love
as we love it.

GRAND COUNCIL FIRE OF
AMERICAN INDIANS, 1927

Earth Awareness

The Earth is alive! This statement is steadily becoming an accepted part of the common knowledge of people worldwide. It is, perhaps, the one piece of truth that serves to unite ancient beliefs about the Earth with the present modern technological society.

It is a view of the Earth's living matter—the oceans, land, and air—as an interacting and self-regulating system, which can be seen as a single living organism. Although the methods by which the concept of the "Living Earth" were come by differ greatly between the Ancients

3

and the Moderns, their effect is the same: a belief in the living Earth strikes an emotional chord in the consciousness of the believers that creates a bond between man and his planet. That bond is the fundamental cause for respect and harmony to exist between humans and Mother Earth, or Gaia, as the Greeks called her over two thousand years ago.

It has not always been this way. A great gap of time has passed between ancient man's perspective of the Earth and the resulting relationship he enjoyed and honored, and modern man's current growing awareness of the same. To the Native Americans of the North American continent, for example, the relationship between man and the Earth was powerful. The wilderness was home. It was their life. It gave them life. All members of other kingdoms were their brothers and sisters. Man was nourished, on all levels of his being, from the powers inherent within the minerals, plants, and animals, which he recognized and respected. Everything from a rock to an eagle belonged to one whole Living Earth. All came forth from one Creator. All were equal in soul and body. Prayer and ceremony that stimulated visions and opened a line of communication were the common tool through which this brotherhood was felt so deeply.

Native Americans left nothing to chance. They called to the rising Sun and called it "Grandfather." They lamented to the Moon and called her "Grandmother." To them, the Earth was "Mother." The life force in everything was celebrated. The powers of Nature were considered superior and were honored ceremonially at times of planting and harvesting. The seas, mountains, seasons, and all the moods of weather were considered far more than mere phenomena of Nature, but as living, conscious forces with whom they sought to coexist in harmony. This interaction accented the unity and beauty of an entire culture. It was a way of life, a philosophy, and a religion all in one.

Such a relationship was not limited to the people of this continent. The Celtics of ancient Britain, the East

Indians, and tribes indigenous to lands worldwide give us evidence of the same values.

Somehow, over time, our relationship with our Earth changed. An unfolding independence and sophistication in the form of technology may be the primary culprit. Changes in the precepts of religion have surely played a major role, as has man's view of himself as the superior creature of all Creation, resulting in an attitude of "separateness" between himself and the "lower" kingdoms of nature. As this gap has widened, evidence of it has become more and more apparent. The dawn of the twenty-first century has brought with it tired and overworked soil, polluted waters, foul air, all the result of the loss of man's kinship with Nature.

Pollution does not occur overnight. Rather, it is both action and inaction over a long period of time that have desecrated the face of our Earth. Our consciousness has shifted, and with it, our values. I think this can be best understood by the tremendous emphasis that has been placed on two things: ownership and profit.

As settlements grew into communities, towns, and cities, man began to place monetary values and boundaries on the land. We desire to own the land and to have houses. Urban development has grown wildly. We have become industrialized. Great financial proceeds have come from the seemingly unquenchable thirst for creating our material empires. Gold, silver, and other minerals have been ripped from the body of the Earth in growing quantities. We have an insatiable need for timber supplies, and as a result, vast areas of our planet have been made bare. The majestic redwood forests of the northwestern United States are being destroyed. The Brazilian rain forest is disappearing at an alarming rate. Whales, eagles, bears, fish, and other wildlife have been pushed, relentlessly, to the brink of extinction to meet the ever-growing needs of our consumer society.

We have poisoned the land with huge amounts of chemicals over the last half century. These chemicals are not selective in the life-forms they kill. Health hazards that threaten plants, animals, and humans alike are continuously coming to light as a result of the overuse and misuse of pesticides. Water pollution has reached frightening proportions. Environmentalists fear that as much as 75 percent of our drinking water supply in the United States may be polluted to some degree. The Atlantic Ocean is no longer hiding the excessive amounts of toxic wastes that have been dumped. The summer of 1988 saw hospital wastes, the decaying bodies of laboratory rats, and garbage of many types wash up all along the eastern shores of the United States. Perhaps nothing in our time has caused us to realize more profoundly that our "out of sight, out of mind" policy regarding waste cannot continue.

There is more. Industrial pollution of all kinds is a growing problem. The Earth's aura continues to be stifled by an increasing envelope of toxic gases and pollutants thrown skyward in ignorance and indifference. You can actually see the effect as sunsets blaze forth with the brilliant reds and golds of a polluted atmosphere more often than from the natural hues of a contented state of Nature. One of the most pressing dangers we face is acid rain. The poisonous gases and pollutants ejected into the atmosphere from the smokestacks of industries, worldwide, are carried by the wind, only to fall back to Earth as nitric and sulfuric rain and snow. This acidic precipitation settles on water and soil, destroying aquatic and plant life with frightening speed. This growing problem is even more serious in Europe than in the United States.

There can be little doubt that if present trends continue, we are in for some real catastrophes that will be irreversible. We must take steps, now, to cease spoilage of our planet. Maybe a good place to start is with a clear understanding of what the word *ecology* really means.

Ecology is the study of the relations between living beings and their environment. An understanding of these interrelationships helps us to see that interdependencies exist, resulting in a whole, connected ecosystem. If we view the Earth as a whole, then we can grasp the reality that the planet and all the life-forms that dwell upon it form one massive ecosystem. In such an ecosystem there is no separateness. One is dependent upon the other. One affects the other. What is good for one is good for all. Likewise, what is bad for one is bad for all. We are simply deceiving ourselves if we think differently. It is this interdependency that we have forgotten or that we choose to ignore. There is more than one villain causing the loss of our memory of the need for balance in our fragile ecosystem.

Religion, in its infancy, was a formal attempt to understand nature so that its path could be tread with confidence. Priests and priestesses of various times and cultures have worked to refine their awareness and understanding of Nature and her laws to an unsurpassable art in which Nature is not the master nor the chela but an ally. Within the harmony created by such a partnership, all things were believed possible. But, in the twentieth century, science became man's religion. Science has come forth as the New Messiah, bringing with it a change in perspective, the birth of technology, and a profound change of values. In answer to the demands of an increasing world population and the means to feed, house, clothe, and provide medicine for it, science has in many ways waged an unceasing war *against* nature. Our physical needs and material wants have pushed science to harness, overcome, or out and out destroy any forces that will not bend to our image of reality. On the one hand, we all enjoy and reap the rewards of technological achievements that have made our lives easier and longer. On the other hand, we all suffer from the wastes of progress that have tainted and fouled our planet and our prospects for future survival.

Thankfully, the Cosmic Law of Cycles is bringing in the winds of change. As the winds begin to blow, they will clear the way for the evidence of our mistakes to speak loud enough for all to hear. Many people, worldwide, have awakened to the signs of ecological imbalance and know in their hearts that it is time to listen to the voices of Nature. It is time, once again, to know the Living Earth as "Mother," as Gaia, before it is too late. Some have come to realize, or perhaps *remember* from the pool of human ancestral memory, that although our attitude of superiority has lulled us into a false sense of security, this must change so that the Earth and all the life kingdoms may survive.

Our present predicament did not come without warning. For example, the Hopi people of northeastern Arizona are known and respected for their prophecies, most of which concern the Earth and its environmental difficulties and geological changes. It is imperative to note that some of these predictions are several hundred years old, uttered in a time before the rivers became sluggish and tainted with the pollution of our progress. The Hopi speak of a time, which many believe is now, when the sons and daughters of the ones who took over their land would come to their Elders to learn of the "old ways" or traditions of the Hopi, as well as of all Indians peoples. That is of living in harmony with Nature, as opposed to challenging her ways to gain technological supremacy. This is happening. People of all ages, from all nations, are seeking knowledge of the Indians' spiritual ways and values, at the forefront of which is the belief that the Earth is alive.

Another fact of the life of the Native American that resulted in a harmony with Nature was and still is a sophisticated knowledge of plants for health and "psychological knowledge of disease cure." Although much of that pure wisdom has been lost or ignored, it is being revived. And it can continue to be revived. We can reach a compatible balance between the forces and values of science and Nature's natural cures. Prevention that can come from Nature is a way to prevent the need and use of sometimes dangerous and harmful modern equipment, drugs, and treatments. We do not have to dismantle science. But neither do we have to destroy Nature. A balance of the old and the new, and moderation, are the keys.

Can we really create a world in which the "new ways" of science and progress can coexist, peacefully, with Nature and life? Can we come to a point where we realize that we *all* share the same future? I believe so. However, several things must be taken into careful consideration. It will take time for the necessary changes to come about. It took a long time for man to "disconnect" himself from Mother Earth. It will take a long time for man to "reconnect" himself. In many ways, the odds we face are great because each of us must be willing to change. Technology exists to provide services and wares for a convenience-minded world. Profit blinds industry and dictates its tactics. Human welfare and survival are placed on a pedestal above all other life kingdoms. The Earth is being used up to fuel the fossil-burning vehicles of our modern society. We create wastes that we have little idea how to rid ourselves of. Neither we nor these circumstances are going to change overnight, no matter, it would seem, how great the risks. Time must be spent in re-educating ourselves about the importance of the *natural* world and its preservation for future generations.

This brings us to another point of change that must occur. We, the residents of Mother Earth, must refine and, in some instances, completely revise our sense of values. Profit need not be a dirty word, or totally sacrificed for a clean and safe environment. At the same time, profit cannot be the absolute end that sanctions any means to its purposes. We must search for ways for profit and Nature to exist, side by side, along with life itself. This balance must then preside as the ethic and value we adopt. It can be done, and we must do it now. We will know our values have changed when the right to life of the great whales, trees, deserts, rivers, and mountains is defended as equally as the right to life for a human being.

Yet another change that must happen involves an honest, clear understanding of the livingness of the Earth. This is one way that we can witness science and Earth awareness working together. In his book *Gaia: A New Look at Life on Earth*, James Lovelock, an independent British scientist whose invention of the electron capture detector revolutionized environmental analysis, has presented society with a new and radically different model of Earth, at least "new" to modern times. Lovelock, relying on information from various scientific disciplines ranging from astronomy to zoology, presents the concept that the Earth's life operates as a single organism that generates conditions that sustain its survival. The hypothesis is that the Earth exists as a complex system, one that has the capacity to keep the planet a "fit place for life." Reading the marvelously researched scientific data that comprise Lovelock's theory makes the bottom line quite clear: The Earth is alive, a living, breathing, evolving organism in which one life affects all others.

We must adopt the attitude and belief that the Living Earth of the American natives, the Celts, Shintos, and many other past cultures is the "Mother." The word *mother* has meaning that reaches into the deepest levels of our inner being, stirring powerful ancient alliances and emotions that speak of *origin* and *source*. Recognition of this fundamental emotion tells us how inseparable man truly is from his planet. Furthermore, the view of Earth as the mother clearly establishes a parent-Earth, child-mankind, relationship. Such a relationship finds the child, mankind, and the other kingdoms protected and provided for by the parent, Earth, a fact recognized and respected, not merely *expected* and taken for granted by our ancestors. Separating ourselves from Nature has created a sense of "independence" from the Earth, resulting, I believe, in virtually all of our present ecological problems.

Aside from being the "provider," Earth was also considered a stern parent who reprimanded her children when they strayed from a loving, peaceful relationship with Nature. We can see evidence of this in the legends of the Hopi people. Their legends tell of three times when the Earth rose up in reproach against her human children. Earthquakes and floods came as punishment to get mankind back on track with natural law. We may be reaching yet another time and need for reprimand, or so it would seem. Any number of current "threats" to the survival of the planet could be touted as dangerous to the continuation of life, ours and the Earth's. The Hopi say that we are in the Fourth World now. One might wonder how long it will be before Mother Earth reprimands her children again. There is mounting geological evidence, aside from man-made environmental problems, that could very well be interpreted in this manner. There is a decided increase in seismic activity, worldwide. Volcanoes erupt with intensity on the North American continent, where such activity is not a part of our usual concerns. Climate changes are being felt with growing alarm as droughts, floods, shorter growing seasons, and erosion challenge us to have to face the fact that our Earth may very well be warning us to get back on track.

Perhaps one of the most profoundly positive beliefs of the Native Americans of North America involves their relationship with the body of the Earth Mother. It can be described as a physical, as well as emotional and certainly spiritual relationship, encompassing and touching all these levels within man's consciousness. In 1981 through 1983, while doing research for *The Earth Changes Survival Handbook*, I investigated the red man's view of the body of the Earth and discovered that there were many places considered sacred by the various tribes over the face of the North American continent, including Canada and Mexico. This fact piqued my curiosity so much that I began a full-fledged pursuit of why this was so. The answer turned out to be twofold. First, the native people knew that the Earth is alive. Second, they believed that the Living Earth energy is stronger in certain areas than in others. They also believed that particular areas, oftentimes mountains, oceans, valleys, and hills, were reservoirs of pure *geopsychic* energy. Such places were intuitively located and experienced by those who were closely connected to the Earth Mother. It was, I believe, that very *connection* between man and Earth that gave the Native Americans such an acute psychic awareness of these power spots in the first place.

Not long after I began my study of Earth awareness, I came to realize that the planetary perspectives of the people native to the North American continent had a great deal in common with those of indigenous people of many other lands. While the ceremonies to celebrate these power spots may differ, as well as the use that was made of the Earth's emanating power, the method by which the knowledge was come by was the same: *intuition*.

The dictionary defines the word *intuition* as the "power to perceive something immediately without special information or reasoning." Ancient people had no intellectual knowledge of the Earth's power flow, for there was none to be had. They knew by the power of their intuitive consciousness and nothing more.

Feng Shui

Since ancient times the Chinese have believed in and practiced a unique and complex system of geomancy called Feng Shui, the Chinese Art of Placement. The term *geomancy* implies the art of divination by means of signs derived from the Earth; in short, by being able to "read" the Earth. Translated to mean wind and water, Feng Shui is based upon the forces the Chinese believed to be responsible for health, prosperity, and good fortune. Although there is still a great deal of mystery surrounding this old art, it continues to be widely practiced today, particularly in Hong Kong.

It is said that Feng Shui evolved from simple observation. In her writing *Feng Shui: The Chinese Art of Placement*, author Sarah Rossbach tells of the observation that "people are affected, for good or ill, by surroundings." Although Feng Shui involves a more inclusive and complex system of energies than that of the Native Americans, the end results are the same. For example, the Feng Shui priests took astrological aspects into consideration, even using the planets to identify shapes in the landscape. A sharp, jagged mountain peak is considered to be masculine and influenced and ruled by the planet Mars, while a well-rounded hill or natural high mound are said to be feminine and ruled by the planet Venus. Special attention is given to shapes in the landscape, such as the course of rivers, and animal shapes appearing in the natural terrain. Malefic animals were the harbingers of ill fortune, while the benefic ones, like the dragon, were the most frequent symbols of protection and good fortune.

The most significant component of Feng Shui is ch'i. Ch'i is best described as the life essence or motivating force in Nature. It is, literally, that which determines the ''livingness'' of the Earth and all forms of life. It is the Earth's blood. Without it, the Earth would not be alive. This life force is constantly changing, contracting and expanding, as the breathing of the planetary lungs might do, spiraling around and around within the body of Mother Earth. On its course through the Earth's form, ch'i rises near the planet's surface in some places and actually protrudes through her crust in others. Such locations give rise to mountains and volcanoes. In areas where ch'i extends deeply below the surface, the land will be dry and flat, the most negative type of terrain. Where ch'i is flowing abundantly, mountains form, trees grow tall and strong, flowers bloom, the air is clean and fresh, and the waters flow clearly and are easily accessible. When ch'i is far away or blocked, stagnation results in sickness and pollution, and the fate of all the life-forms in the area will tend to be negative.

The Native Americans must have known of ch'i to have designated particular areas as ''sacred.'' We can surely interpret this as an awareness of the flow of the blood of the Earth, perhaps concentrated in certain places which, in turn, became the chosen locations of their medicine wheels, cairns, ceremonial lodges and sites. We also know that the Indian people took great care to orient the openings of their dwellings and sacred lodges to the east, symbolizing the homage paid to Ancient Grandfather Sun, and capturing the first fresh light power of the new dawn. In this way, celestial influences did indeed play a role in their perspective and level of awareness, as it did with the Chinese.

Practitioners of Feng Shui say that the Earth's ch'i can be tapped in a manner somewhat similar to an acupuncturist being able to tap the ch'i of a human being. All components of the environment, so it is said, affect the flow of ch'i, especially trees, buildings, water, even the

Sun. When an area is not balanced due to its ch'i not flowing smoothly, measures can be taken to correct the situation. These measures include reshaping the terrain or a building to promote a more proper flow of the life force. I have wondered if piles of stones called cairns or circles of stones of both the prehistoric Celts and the Native Americans might have, in part, served a similar purpose. Perhaps the circle itself captured the energy of a power spot, causing it to move in a circular motion, long considered a powerful and natural movement and the oldest, most sacred symbol known to man.

Further evidence of the Earth awareness of Native Americans can be seen in the way they marked their special locations with stones. We do not know, for certain, the total extent of their motives, but it is believed that stone circles, dolmens, and standing stones were placed on the Earth in particular spots for specific reasons. Colin Wilson's comments in his book *Mysteries* may give us a clue. Let us suppose that standing stones, their heels buried in the soil, act as acupuncture-type "needles." Wilson notes: "But the chief clue to their actual use comes from Standing Rock, in South Dakota, a megalith against which Sioux Indian medicine men used to press their spines to *revitalize* (italics mine) their powers of telepathy, healing, and second sight."

It is interesting how this passage from *Mysteries* makes such a clear statement as to how Earth energy may affect the human psyche. If the megaliths that Wilson talks about, many of which were single standing stones, were used in this fashion by some Indian medicine people, then they may very well have been used in the same way by those who set such megaliths throughout the British Isles and Europe hundreds of centuries ago. And it is then safe to say that the places the Native Americans considered to be Sacred Sites were powerful sources of energy that had a definite and pronounced effect on the quantity and quality of the shaman's powers. The shamans were the channels for the energy and knew how to tap it, drawing it into their bodies, processing it and transmitting it for a variety of purposes ranging from healing, making rain, conversing with spirits, to fore-telling the future.

Discovering Sacred Earth Power

By taking Wilson's comments another step, we can be-lieve that Earth energy was, and is, a tremendous source of spiritual development. It is a source for promoting vitality and good health on all levels of the human body and consciousness. Having the Native Americans' intui-tive skill to discover such locations in any given area would surely be desirable. I have come to realize that not only did our ancestors, worldwide, seek out and find these powerful "hot spots," but that they were the sites for building medicine wheels, megalithic circles, pyramids, and temples. Sometimes these man-made "markers" served the role of siphoning Earth energy from deep within the body of the planet, making use of the endless fountain of power.

We know that these "sacred" places also served as sites of ceremony. As said earlier, Native Americans took nothing in Nature for granted nor left anything to chance. They took measures that were highly esoteric to contact and connect with the "spirits" of nature to help insure that the Sun would rise, rain would come, and that the souls of the dead would guide and protect their way of life. Each major event during the ceremonial year, namely planting and harvesttime, was marked by cere-monies designed to invoke cooperation from the spirits of Nature. A ceremony was an inherited rite passed down from generations before, many of which are still prac-ticed today among tribes across the North American con-tinent. Because of the power that flows from the Earth's body, ceremonies were held at the high-energy spots within the area the tribe inhabited. The force of the ceremony would be greatly intensified as a result.

Sacred Sites were also used as astronomical observa-tories. These observatories, composed of stone calen-dars, were erected throughout the world. In recent years a whole new science has been born around this investigation. Much research is currently being done to further determine the astronomical use of megalithic sites throughout North America and Europe. Archaeoastronomy relies upon a combination of archeology and astronomy. It seeks to discover to which planets or stars, phases of the Moon and/or Sun, the various stone circles were aligned. From this, archaeoastronomers hope to learn what degree of astronomical sophistication the Ancients may have possessed. The most celebrated attempt to date that may yield answers to this question is seen in Gerald Hawkins's book *Stonehenge Decoded*. In it, a new perspective of that prehistoric monument being an ancient observatory is brought to light.

An exciting order of thoughts begins to emerge from our discussion thus far. Early man believed the Earth was alive. He was able, through his close, intuitive relationship with the planet, to seek out and tap the emanating Earth energies to inspire him and to awaken his psychic faculties, which he used to gain an even deeper relationship with the spirits and forces of all of Nature. Upon these same power spots he built his circles and temples of worship. He erected calendars that may have been used not only to mark time, but to "connect" with celestial forces far beyond the Earth and outside himself. That is *spiritual technology* in the profoundest sense.

Politics of the Environment

We have seen that there is a need for change. We know of the increasing evidence that is mounting regarding our negative environmental affairs. We are all aware of groups and organizations, such as Green Peace and Friends of the Earth, that have been formed all over the world, to address various environmental issues, combat them, and educate our global society as to our plight. Some of these groups already have, and continue to, make a difference.

It is precisely due to this grass roots ecological movement that the American government has had to take notice. Recognition occurred several years ago with the formation of the Environmental Protection Agency. Although there are many pros and cons about any real good coming from the rules and activities of the EPA, and many questions go unanswered, it is still a step in the right direction. But neither environmental groups nor governments can do it all. We must all cooperate. We must join the growing collective body of people dedicated to bringing about global change. It is true that there is power in numbers. As the numbers grow, so will our voice. We can lobby, we can vote, and we can stay informed. Above all, we must make a commitment and stick to it.

As individuals, we can each make an effort to reconnect ourselves to the Earth. We must rediscover what we have lost, and in order for it to have any real value, it must be a personal discovery. Cultivating a closer relationship with Mother Earth is entirely subjective. Some may choose to spend more time out-of-doors. Some may choose to join or even organize a group that focuses upon some specific or general environmental issue. Some may educate others. All of us must become living examples of our ability to change. We can work on creating and developing a relationship with the Earth, as we would a human friend. By learning how to "read" the Earth, to detect her energy spots and use the energy of those sacred places as the Ancients did, we can awaken our intuition for greater planetary awareness and better self-awareness as well.

In the next chapter I will give you the necessary tools for this purpose. Earth energies are complex, as are the life systems of all living organisms. There is, therefore, a need to simplify our awareness and understanding of those energies. I feel that the easiest way to grasp them is to divide them into three groups: *electricity, magnetism*, and *electromagnetism*. By knowing the unique qualities of each of these Life Energies, you will more easily recognize and establish a conscious reaction to every place you go. You will develop an understanding of your reactions and come to know how Earth energies affect your body and health, your emotions, mind, and soul. You will learn how to locate power spots or natural Earth vortices and know what kind of energy they emit. You will learn how to "read" nature, and in doing so, gain a better awareness of which areas of the Earth are best for you and why.

Discovering the Living Earth

This is not just another book about ecology. It is a book about *discovery* of the Living Earth. It is written for the purpose of helping you regain the connection with your home. It is, furthermore, a book designed to help you enjoy the fruits of the labors of the Creator that are common in value to us all.

Because travel is so easy today, many of us are embarking upon journeys to lands worldwide. Many of these are trips to sacred places. Some make such journeys as personal spiritual "pilgrimages" to touch into past life locations and experiences, while others seek out the "energy" in Sacred Sites and/or vortices all over the globe for healings, visions, and inspiration.

The Earth's power and beauty are a constant source of wonder. Our quest for the solitude of her power in the prairies, mountains, valleys, and seas fills our heart with the power of her life force as it flows through her veins, empowering her body and ours.

If we are to regain our connection with the Earth, we must come to know her power, intimately. That requires us to cultivate much more than ecological awareness in the form of statistical knowledge. We must develop *ecological consciousness*. As we do this, one more mind and attitude will change, and mankind, collectively, will be one step closer to a healthier, more complete relationship with our planet.

I have selected five countries to explore for their Sacred Sites and vortices. I have sought to categorize these places by the *Life Energy* inherent in each. They are all filled with living, sacred Earth power. Together, they are regions that cover huge areas of terra firma, where man and civilizations have been born and have flourished for centuries. These places are held in esteem not only for their appeal to general tourism, but because they are places singled out so often for spiritual pilgrimages. Above all, these locations provide power and refuge for the traveler, as well as for the truth seeker interested in learning greater Earth awareness and connection. They are a wonderfully exciting cross section by which we can view and measure the whole Living Earth. The lands I have selected are the United States, England, India, Tibet, and Egypt.

We will explore each of these lands from the perspective of its geographical location, terrain, human history, religion, and culture. We will determine whether each is electric, magnetic, or electromagnetic. A map of each country will serve as a guideline as to the location of the vortices and Sacred Sites and will also offer an indication of the *major* connecting lines of force known as leys.

We can come to know the Earth as *mother* again. We can and we must . . . before it is too late.

CHAPTER TWO

LIFE ENERGIES:
Electricity, Magnetism, and Electromagnetism

To see the world in a grain of sand
And a heaven in a wild flower;
Hold infinity in the palm of your hand
And eternity in an hour.

WILLIAM BLAKE
Auguries of Innocence

Energy

Science tells us that all is *energy*. The dictionary defines energy as, "the material power of the universe." Since everything in the macrocosm is material, no matter what its form, then this definition suggests that energy is its animating power. In my view, energy is life force, the prana of the Cosmos. In order to truly comprehend the reality of the "Living Earth," I believe that we must come to view the planet as one organism of energy, a unit complete and whole. The energies of all living bodies are multiple and varied, but they exist in a balanced and harmonious symphony of *wholeness*, as suggested by James Lovelock's Gaia hypothesis mentioned earlier. Gaining a clearer understanding of *wholeness* is an

20

integral part of the process of reconnecting ourselves to the Earth. The implications of this concept are profound.

In the halls of science the theory of wholeness rests most solidly on the shoulders of renowned physicist David Bohm. Bohm, a contemporary of Albert Einstein, proposed a revolutionary supposition that he labeled "implicate order." In this, Bohm has devised virtually an entirely new map of the universe designed to create a different understanding of our world. His theory has stirred a lot of controversy not only because of its revolutionary ideas but also, perhaps, due to its opposition to diehard premises so deeply ingrained in science. Since the time of Aristotle, science has maintained that Nature can and must be analyzed in parts. Bohm says different. His theory proposes that the universe be considered as an *undivided whole*. Neither Bohm, nor others who have reached the same conclusion, have succeeded in changing science's persistence in dealing with the universe in bits and pieces. "Wholeness," Bohm points out, "is one of those ideas almost everyone pays lip service to but virtually no one takes seriously enough to find out what it means. For to undertake wholeness seriously is to make an incredible journey, abandoning everything that is familiar and comfortable. It is as weird as the idea of slipping through to the other side of a mirror."

In seeking to give Bohm's theory careful consideration, we discover that, in essence, it originates within the so-called quantum world, the subatomic realm of existence. In this realm of reality, for example, two entities at *any* distance from each other have an effect on each other, implying that they are united even though they appear separate. Another way that this theory has been expressed is found in the language of the "new" physics, which states that the "observer" affects what he "observes." In this, observer and observed are found to be somehow merging or, truer still, *merged* all along. An acceptance of Bohm's hypothesis abolishes separateness completely and unites the Cosmos into a wholeness, changing the old views forever. Because of this, the scientific community, at large, is not rushing to embrace a view that would require such a complete rewriting of the textbooks.

Another reason that the scientific community is reluctant to rush into acceptance of Bohm's or any other theory of wholeness is the fact that the concept of wholeness is, traditionally, a mystical one. "All is one" and "I Am" are esoterically based phrases that have been repeated time and time again to explain and affirm the state of wholeness that *is*. Spiritual disciplines of both the East and the West have long sought to impart that knowledge and the experience of the at-one-ment of all that exists. Although the gap between science and mysticism is narrowing somewhat, it is still there. This makes it difficult, at best, to look to or rely upon either science or religious and spiritual affirmation for confirmation of the truth of wholeness. In any case, it is far better to *experience* it for ourselves. The words of the Great Lord Buddha serve us well in this quest: "Believe not a thing because another man hath said it. Believe it only when you have experienced it and know it to be truth."

In seeking our individual experience with the Earth and her energies, we need, first, to acquaint ourselves with her physical body. Our planet is so beautiful. Dense, fragrant forests and majestic, snow-capped peaks are found worldwide. Rivers, lakes, and the great oceans bless all life-forms with their nourishing substance and beauty. Anyone who has stood on the rim of the Grand Canyon has not only beheld the beauty there but has also felt the quiet power of Mother Earth and Nature.

Behind the planet's physical beauty there lies *energy*. It is this energy that the people of past ages knew of and sought out. In trying to deal with and relate to the forces in Nature, they chose to personify these energies as gods and goddesses and powerful spirits whom they associated with the winds, trees, rivers, mountains, and stones. The abodes of the spirits were considered sacred and were often the sites of ceremony, vision quests, burial, and replenishment of power.

While the beliefs and practices of ancient people may not totally comprise our degree of Earth awareness today, it can contribute greatly to it. We live in a different world. Our challenges are not the same. We are caught up in the fever of our modern times and the problems it presents to us. While the "back to basics" slogans emerging out of the turbulent sixties did stir our concern and capture our attention, they are not enough. I believe our concern will grow and intensify when we are able, as individuals, to go beyond the physical beauty of our planet and connect with those underlying *energies*.

When we accept the truth that all is energy, we begin to have a clearer awareness and subsequent understanding that although there is *One Source*, there are many manifestations of it. Shortly before his death, Albert Einstein was working fervently to discover what he called a Unified Field Theory that would *prove* "One Source" . . . uniting all the manifestations of it. Every form emanates its own unique energy vibration, giving rise to the illusion of separateness.

As I mentioned earlier, in my personal attempt to understand the manifestations of the universal nature of energy, I have divided them into three categories: electricity, magnetism, and electromagnetism. These terms are borrowed from science, but in this context they do not necessarily adhere to strict scientific definition. Rather, they serve the purpose of categorizing the energy of the Earth's body and aura (atmosphere) into easily identifiable qualities. I feel that these qualities lend themselves equally in describing not only the nature of the Earth's body, but also the life-forms within each kingdom, including human personality and behavior, weather, our diets, indeed, all aspects of manifested life. Therefore, I consider the three as "Life Energies" that emanate from the *indwelling power* in *all* forms.

As we explore each of these Life Energies, we will begin to see the very nature of Reality unfold. We will evaluate each Life Energy, paying close attention to the quality or "charge" each possesses, how that "charge" manifests in Nature, and what effect it has on our human bodies and consciousness. This will provide a system by which we can "read" or interpret the Earth's bodily power and come to recognize how the Earth is affecting us on all levels of our being: physically, emotionally, mentally, and spiritually. We have already taken a close critical look at how we have affected our planet. Perhaps if we come to realize, consciously, how the Earth affects us, we can come closer to creating a healthier and wiser respect for the powers inherent in both.

Electricity as Life Energy

Electricity is the first of the Life Energies we shall investigate. It is the male force in Nature and is responsible for all procreation. Electricity is described as possessing the attributes of vitality, aggression, birth, and is extremely and powerfully active, animating *forms* in the Cosmos. In this view, electricity would not be unlike what the Taoists call ch'i. In the book *Tao Magic*, Laszlo Legeza describes ch'i as "the Vital Spirit, [that] fills the world of the Taoist." The author goes further to describe that ch'i infuses everything and, in doing so, gives energy to man, as well as life and movement to Nature.

There are three major sources of electricity within the Earth's body and aura: volcanoes, lightning, and deserts. This means that all active volcanoes and volcanic terrains, such as lava fields and flows and underground lava rivers, are electrical in Nature. It also implies that mountains and mountain ranges, worldwide, are electrical in and of themselves, no matter what the nature of their surrounding areas, with a few exceptions which I shall point out later. The higher the mountain(s), the more electrical it is. An active volcano is the most electrical, dormant ones, have less intensity, and extinct volcanoes have the least charge. It is all a matter of degrees. Hot geysers such as those found in Yellowstone National Park in Wyoming are also quite electrical, as is the Earth's core.

There is also electrical climate, found, for the most part, in desert terrains. Deserts are hot and arid, sometimes accompanied by mountains, which add an even stronger electrical charge to the area. While all locations around the globe receive lightning as a part of passing weather systems, areas that are prone to frequent and intense lightning are recipients of surges of atmospheric electricity, again, adding electrical intensity during such occurrences.

Lightning occurs when the electrical field in the Earth's aura becomes so strong that the insulating capability of the air breaks down. A bolt of lightning is a sudden flow, mostly of negative charge, from a cloud to the ground. Lightning is truly a powerful phenomenon of nature. At its peak current, it can carry a voltage of two hundred thousand amperes or more, with the associated temperatures rising to millions of degrees! Because of this heat, the air explosively expands and contracts, producing pressure pulses that are heard as thunder. There are approximately eighteen hundred thunderstorms in progress at any given time over some area of the Earth's surface, evidence of the planet's production of replenishing electrical power.

Yet another atmospheric phenomenon that contributes to the amount and quality of electricity we receive on the Earth is known as the Van Allen belts. Believed to be composed of charged particles emitted during intense solar radiation and penetrating the upper atmosphere, these belts, two of which have been observed, are responsible for sudden variations in the intensity of the Earth's magnetic field. This results in so-called magnetic storms, as well as auroral displays such as the northern lights. This brings me to point out that the Sun, of course, is the most powerful source of electricity that affects our planetary ecosystem, although it is completely objective of it.

Desert terrain is shaped by the wind currents and the waters of the ancient past and present. In fact, hot, dry winds are another source of electrical Life Energy, such as the foehn winds and "witch" winds of Europe, and the chinooks that blow over the Great Plains of North America. Our deserts are growing in size. During the last fifty years, the size of both sand-covered lands and great areas of rocky, sun-scorched soil that cannot support human life have increased. In the last fifty-eight years, approximately 450,000 square miles have been added to the Sahara, due to a combination of natural forces and man's farming, grazing, and removal of resources to gather fuel. As the deserts grow, the planet's climate changes, and if it continues, it will cause problems. We need plants that the desert is devoid of for proper balance in our atmosphere to be maintained. Deserts will not grow crops without unique farming techniques that are difficult, at best.

The soil in electrical areas tends to be mostly sandy and acidic, and it must be mulched thoroughly prior to the planting of most crops. The most common plants for electrical soils are those that require little water and/or those that have long tap roots or are capable of creating their own internal aquifers for water storage.

Areas in the United States that are electrical include: the Sonoran and Mojave deserts of the great Southwest, the Mountains of the Cascade Range (because they are volcanic), the Tetons, the Baja Peninsula, some areas of the Great Plains and the Midwest, and most large cities. Cities "electrify" a given area due to the constant activity, both positive and negative, that goes on and because of the concentration of life, fuel consumption, and energy generated. So the electricity generated by a city, with occasional exceptions, will overpower the natural terrain and electrify an area. When large cities are found in places that are naturally electrical, the degree of intensity involved can prove to be truly strong.

Electricity affects our human physical, emotional, mental, and spiritual levels of body and consciousness. Physically, electricity charges up the body, revitalizing it with surges of Life Energy. When one is tired from overwork or low on physical energy for some other reason, being in an electrical location on the Earth helps tremendously to replenish the body's strength and vigor. One must be cautious, however, for too great a surge of electricity will tend to elevate the blood pressure, increase the heart rate, and cause an intensification of tension and stress which can negatively affect the nervous system. Common "electrical ailments" from an overabundance of electricity are: anxiety and other stress-related problems, hypertension, heart palpitations, as well as fevers and a proneness to inflammations and arthritis. Too much electricity adversely affects and can cause stiffness and pain in the bones, especially the joints, resulting in arthritic-type conditions.

Emotionally, electrical Life Energy intensifies what we are feeling, positive or negative, resulting in exuberance and joy, or giving our anxieties and anger a much sharper edge. Whether we apply it to the emotional or mental level of ourselves, electricity intensifies us. It can cause the mind and intellect to be more alert, to think more quickly, and to grasp ideas and process them faster. Spiritually, electrical energy will inspire and uplift us. It can give us deeper insight and awareness by triggering an "awakening" of the higher yet more subtle levels of our consciousness, such as intuition. Ultimately electricity, when utilized properly, can awaken the soul itself into *conscious* activity.

Magnetism as Life Energy

Let us now turn our attention to *magnetism*. Magnetism, for all practical purposes, is the opposite of electricity. Whereas electricity is the male force in Nature, magnetism is the feminine. The female force in Nature is responsible for the creation of the *forms* that house all lives. The greatest source of magnetic Life Energy is water, in the form of seas, rivers, lakes, precipitation, and underground aquifers and springs. Therefore, land nearby and/or such water sources are magnetic in charge.

Magnetic soil, as a rule, is black, rich, and highly fertile. Tropical areas are a good example. Tropical storms such as cyclones, hurricanes, and typhoons breed in the low-latitude belts over the oceans, bringing with them warm, torrential magnetic downpours. Coastal areas, some islands, and marshlands and low-country swamps are all highly magnetic. The most variable and the most remarkable of atmospheric trace gases is water vapor. In its various forms, water vapor controls the behavior of the air surrounding the Earth, and this great source of magnetism is responsible for the virtual stability of our global ecosystem.

Magnetism, like electricity, has an effect on the human body and consciousness. Physically, it promotes relaxation of the nerves and muscles, causing a release of tension and a reduction of stress. Too much magnetism can have negative physical results due to the "slowing down" effects it can have. Common negative ailments are depression, sluggish digestion, poor circulation, low blood pressure, and retention of body fluids and toxins. Emotionally, magnetism is at its strongest. It deepens our feelings, promoting greater sensitivity. It turns us inward. That, too, of course, may be positive or negative depending upon our own individual response to the depth experienced. On the mental level, magnetism calms and relaxes the mind, particularly the subconscious, and induces dreams, visions, telepathy, and various forms of so-called psychic capabilities. Meditation and prayer become easier and more powerful. People who live in highly magnetic areas tend to put greater emphasis, either mentally and/or spiritually, on beliefs and practices based on psychic phenomena. In fact, in its effect on the higher spiritual planes of our consciousness, magnetism causes us to be more receptive to outside influences and, as a result, to be more affected by them.

Magnetism is pure creative force, operating subjectively, and manifesting as talents and skills ranging from various forms of artistic achievement to musical and poetic attributes. People involved in such endeavors would do well to seek out magnetic places in which to do their work.

Areas of the United States that are quite magnetic include most of Florida, including the Florida Keys, the entire Atlantic seacoast, the coastal areas (only) of the Great Lakes, the swamps of the South, and places near large lakes and rivers.

Electromagnetism as Life Energy

The last of the three Life Energies is *electromagnetism*. As one might readily discern, electromagnetism is a combination of both electricity and magnetism, locked in a compatible state of being. An important point is that when electromagnetic energy isn't in balance, it will behave according to whatever aspect of its energy is the *strongest*. Its weakest component will dwindle and eventually stagnate, and in extreme instances, become nonexistent. For example: If the electric side of electromagnetic energy is stronger, the magnetic side will be greatly diminished or die, resulting in a blockage of the flow or a complete loss of the magnetism. Whether or not this blockage occurs at a specific place on the Earth or in a human body, the results will be the same. A loss of magnetism blocks creative energy, causing infertility. It blocks feeling. It inhibits circulation of life force.

There are a number of things that can cause the imbalance of electromagnetic Life Energy. One of the most common is the presence of a city. As mentioned earlier, cities are quite electric and can diminish the magnetism of an electromagnetic location or cause a totally magnetic area to become electric. On the other hand, profound changes in long-range weather patterns can cause imbalance, as can pollution, or any sort of interruption or interference with the natural balance of a given area.

In its proper state, electromagnetism is a balance of two Life Energies that are the polar opposites of each other, and it is natural healing power. Its healing quality can and does affect every level of the body and consciousness of a human being, the Earth, or members of the other life kingdoms.

A typical electromagnetic terrain has a stable water source and good annual rainfall. It can be flat and/or mountainous, with lots of vegetation and, generally, four full seasons of climate. Usually the water source will be a river, a good-sized lake, or even a large waterfall. In the United States, electromagnetic environments include the Blue Ridge, Smoky, Appalachian, and Rocky Mountain regions, northern Arizona, northern Colorado and California, Yellowstone, the Great Lakes, most of New England, and the Pacific Northwest, including all of Alaska. Several of the Hawaiian Islands are electromagnetic, particularly Maui, for they are half-desert and half-tropical.

Electromagnetic areas are more plentiful than either the electric or magnetic ones. Perhaps this is one of the reasons why our nation is so rich in good land and natural resources. I might also add that the vast majority of Canada is electromagnetic. With these basic attributes of the three Life Energies in mind, you can easily classify any area of the Earth's body into one of the categories. You can also know what effect the Living Earth's energy is having on body, mind, and soul. Being conscious of such effects is a major step toward better planetary awareness.

People and Life Energy

Aside from serving as a tool of Earth awareness, the Life Energies System can be used to categorize people as well. There are individuals who are "electric" in body and personality and who, as a result, are prone to electrical ailments and personal problems. Electrical persons are rather aggressive to varying degrees, outspoken, and very strong-willed, which usually gives a sharp edge to their personality and a degree of determination. Such people are apt to be quite impulsive and always ready to spring into action to fight for a cause and get things done. They are usually fearless and independent, and will go into situations, sometimes treacherous ones, with firm conviction and valor. Perhaps the negative attributes of an electrical personality are the strong tempers that must be controlled and the tendency to jump into situations without careful planning and forethought. They are also quite impatient and restless.

Electrical people possess a lot of power. Learning to

use that power properly is the lesson to be learned. When the indwelling electrical energy is not understood and channeled properly, one or more of the electrical ailments mentioned earlier is likely to manifest. There is no doubt that electrical power, particularly when one is conscious of it, can be a tremendous tool of personal action and achievement. It is the power to get things done. It is the power of the hero and the warrior. It is the power to instigate, and often manifests as the pioneering spirit.

Magnetic people could not be more different. Whereas the electrical personality is quick, powerful, and truly extroverted, the magnetic one is easygoing, calm, much slower to act and react, and often introverted. Of all the qualities inherent in magnetic personalities, their *sensitivity* is the most profound. That sensitivity can manifest either positively or negatively, depending on the many factors involved. Magnetic people express emotion and tend to view life, themselves, and other people from the perspective of their feelings. They are easygoing and usually have a calming effect on others. Their gentleness is definitely an asset. However, magnetic personalities can be weak-willed and often too easily influenced by others and objective influences and conditions. Unlike the electrical personality, they are not fighters.

While the electric person tends to rely heavily on the intellect, education, and a sharp, skilled mind, the magnetic individual is more psychic. They possess subjective skills such as telepathy, vivid and often prophetic dreams, clairvoyance, and/or experience rather frequent out-of-body events during either the waking or sleeping state. Intuition is their most useful and powerful tool of growth once they come to recognize it.

Magnetic people are also very creative, but they use their creative ability in a way that is different from other personality types. They are capable of converting their magnetic energy *into words and sounds*, often making them fine writers and poets, and giving them an excellent sense of rhythm and musical talent. They have a keen sense of color that can lead them into some form of artistic expression such as painting or sculpting.

Emotional balance and battling "dependency" are the wars the magnetic personality must wage in order to grow. Because of their deep sensitivity, that war is not always easy.

Electromagnetic personalities possess both an electric and magnetic side to their nature. As a result, they depend *equally* on their mind and their feelings. They have the ability to work hard and accomplish a great deal, but they also know how to leave the work at the office and go home to relax. They often manifest *skills*, which have been learned and cultivated, side by side with natural *talents*. Furthermore, the electromagnetic personality can be independent or dependent, depending upon the circumstance and the individual's response to it.

Balance is the key word. A formidable task for electromagnetic personalities is to keep each side of their nature equal in power. For example, when, the electrical side is the strongest, then the magnetic nature will be stifled. When this occurs, the person's sensitivity and creativity are blocked. Their dreams can become extremely intense, often resulting in nightmares, and/or increased introversion, causing an inability to communicate or even understand what they feel. Electromagnetic people have excellent physical recuperative powers and are, as a rule, our natural healers. If the magnetic side is strongest, then the electric nature will be stifled. In this case, willpower may be weakened, and the person is less likely to take initiatives. There may even be a tendency toward manipulation and domination when the lack of power is sensed.

Perhaps the most difficult thing that electromagnetic people have to come to grips with is the presence of a *duality* of life energies in their natural makeup. As a result, they often "feel" or "hear" their inner voice giving conflicting thoughts, ideas, and/or opinions. This often leads to an inner conflict and indecision that can be difficult to bring into balance. Resolving inner conflicts is, I feel, the single most rewarding growth experience that the electromagnetic personality has to learn.

Electromagnetic illnesses often have to do with chemical or hormonal imbalances in the physical body. Imbalances that lead to problems such as obesity, bulimia, and anorexia can be fairly common. It is safe to assume that general electromagnetic illnesses will manifest according to which side (electric or magnetic) of the Life Energy duality is weakest.

The three personality types we've discussed respond very differently to planetary energies. For example, if an "electrical" person lives in an electrical location such as high mountains or a city, the intensity of the person's electricity will be greatly enhanced. There's no problem as long as the intensity is controlled, but that isn't easy to maintain over a long period of time. Electrical health and/or emotional difficulties will be the result.

If a magnetic person lives or spends long periods of time in highly magnetic locations, the person's magnetism will also be increased. This can result in an intensification of his already sensitive nature. Too much magnetism can lead to lethargy. A feeling of being overwhelmed, defeated, or having no motivation, except possibly regarding self, is also common.

Electric people need magnetism to balance them out. Living in a magnetic place is one way to accomplish this. On the other hand, magnetic people need electricity. So living in electric places will compensate well. Electromagnetic persons do best in electromagnetic areas, for they promote a more promising opportunity for sustained balance.

Food and Life Energy

The same holds true for diet. As we take in food, we take in the energy inherent in that food. An electric person needs magnetic foods and some electromagnetic ones. Magnetic people need electrical foods. Electromagnetic people do best on a well-rounded electromagnetic diet. I am providing a list of the major foods we consume under the headings of their proper Life Energy.

ELECTRIC FOODS

red meat (lamb, pork, beef, and poultry)
citrus (oranges, lemon, grapefruit, tangelos, tangerines)
wheat, barley, millet
corn
sunflowers
dairy products
ice cream
caffeine
sugar

MAGNETIC FOODS

all vegetables (those that grow under the ground are the
   most magnetic)
beans, peas
rice
water (pure spring)
melons (canteloupe, watermelon, casaba, etc.)
kelp and other seaweeds
berries
grapes
soy

ELECTROMAGNETIC FOODS

fish, shellfish
apples
pears
plums
pineapple
peaches
most nuts

If we come to understand and use this system for "reading the Earth" for deciding where we spend most of our time and what we eat, we can be sure of a more proper balance of our personal Life Energy. We will also possess a much better connection and harmony with Nature and the Earth.

CHAPTER THREE

LIVING EARTH SYSTEMS:
Vortices, Ley Lines, and Sacred Sites

Within and around the Earth, within and around
the hills, within and around the mountain,
your authority returns to you.

A TEWA PRAYER

Earth's Energies

As we have seen, the Living Earth is made up of three
basic Life Energies: electricity, magnetism, and electromagnetism. And we now know how each of these energies affects us physically, emotionally, mentally, and
spiritually. Applying the system of Life Energies to the
whole Earth gives us a clearer picture of the forces generated by our planet and can help us to discover where
the emission sites of those forces are located. The feature
that sets apart Sacred Sites from all others has to do with
these vibrations or Life Energies, but the vibrations
themselves are made up of several components. One
would certainly be their energy charge. Another may be
the presence of either positive or negative ions.

Basically, an ion is an atom, or group of chemically
bonded atoms, that have gained or lost one or more elec-
trons, thus carrying a positive or negative electrical

charge. Research has shown that exposure to a large amount of positive ions can have a negative effect on human health, while negative ions affect health in a positive way. This may explain why certain geographical areas have an influence on one's general health and well-being.

In her monumental work *Earth Wisdom*, Delores LaChapelle points out: "Mountains rise higher into the atmosphere than the surrounding land and are subject to more solar energy and cosmic ray energy from space." Mountaintops, which are highly electrical in nature, are areas where there is an abundance of negative ions, as are places where there are high amounts of vegetation, waterfalls, rapidly moving water such as oceans and rivers, and forests. These sites would have a strongly positive effect on body and consciousness and many such areas are respected as power spots to Native Americans or other cultures who are particularly sensitive to earth energies.

Yet another quality inherent in a Sacred Site involves shapes in the landscape. Here I must refer again to Feng Shui, for shapes do indeed play a major role in not only the good and proper flow of ch'i or Earth blood but also, in and of itself, are believed to be responsible for good or ill fortune. A mountain shaped like a sharp tooth, for example, is thought to have a negative influence on those who live too near it and mountains or hills that "enclose" a house too much will prevent the wind from cleansing the air around the dwelling, resulting in stagnant ch'i and ill-health.

Mountains or hills with flat-tops are considered to be particularly devoid of ch'i, as mountain peaks are the points where heaven and earth come together and from which energy radiates out in all directions. A flat plain that is lacking in water is also devoid of ch'i, as is a straight or fast-moving river.

Aside from particular designs in the landscape, Feng Shui practitioners also honor animal shapes. For example: the dragon embodies a powerful energy to the Chinese and is the symbol of royalty and the source of health and good luck. Finding a dragon shape in the landscape, most frequently in mountain ridges, would be a desirable residence site, for the dragon can ward off sickness and famine and bad luck. A terrestrial contour shaped like a dog may guard the home and its occupants, while a tiger or bear are threatening.

While all the above-mentioned qualities surely contribute to the special energies recognized at a Sacred Site, there is more. Sacred Sites, more often than not, are natural energy *vortices*.

Vortices in the Living Earth

A *vortex* is a mass of energy that moves in a rotary or whirling motion, causing a depression or vacuum at the center. In order to understand more clearly what a vortex is in relation to the Earth, we can compare the planet's body to our own human one. Esoteric teachings tell us that behind the purely physical form there is yet another, more subtle body, known as the etheric double. There are two distinguishing features regarding this body, generally thought of as the *vital* body or form. One is that the seven chakras or sacred centers are located there. Chakras are the main energy points of the etheric body, and they serve the purpose of taking in energy that nourishes the physical body and consciousness. They also emit energy that reflects one's inner life force. The etheric body also contains many acupuncture points, which are somewhat like "lesser chakras." These are tiny openings through which the energy or ch'i of the human body may be tapped and/or manipulated to promote a better flow of Life Energy for maintaining good health. These centers of force can also be applied to the planet.

The etheric body of the Earth functions in the same way as our human one. It serves the same purpose for our planet by being the "vehicle" for the flow of ch'i through the Earth's physical form. Within the planetary body there are acupuncturelike points, and these are the *vortices*. Vortices can be tapped by man not only to prompt a good and powerful flow of Earth energy, but also to use the energy for triggering higher levels of awareness and even altered states of consciousness.

Regarding this, I am reminded of the megalithic standing stones the shaman used for revitalizing his power. Vortices, I came to understand, are places where the planet's energy is closest to the surface and where it is exceptionally strong. Vortices are located all over the Earth, including the oceans and atmosphere as well as on dry land. These powerful eddies of pure Earth power manifest as spiral-like coagulations of energy that are either electric, magnetic, or electromagnetic qualities of life force.

Sedona, Arizona, is an ideal example of vortices because all three Life Energy types are to be found here. There are seven natural Earth vortex sites located in the general Sedona area. Five of them have an electric charge, one is magnetic, and one is electromagnetic. Because of the number of vortices in such a relatively small area and the presence of all three types of energies in these residing power centers, Sedona is unique to this continent and one of the few such locations on the entire planet. Further information about the locations, Life Energy charge, and legends that concern the seven Sedona vortices is located in Chapter 4.

There is a distinguishing point to be made concerning vortices and Sacred Sites, because they are not *necessarily* the same thing. Vortices, as a rule, are natural configurations of pure geomantic energy. But it is also true that human events or the building of structures or markers from highly charged elements of the landscape, such as rocks, can result in a man-made vortex of energy. For the purpose of our discussion, however, we will focus on the purely natural vortices.

Electrical Vortices

When we think back to our definition of the three Life Energies and apply them to the concept of vortices, we

can draw the following conclusions: Electrical vortices
have the effect of physically charging one's energy. These
are excellent places to go when one is low on physical
vitality or in need of inspiration. Spiritual faculties can
also be stimulated at such sites, often stirring the consciousness to the point of opening a clear channel through
which intuitive information can be received. I believe
that such spiritual awakenings can be triggered in electrical vortex areas, whether one is conscious of the pre-
siding power of the area or not.

Sacred Mountains

Some of the most significant locations throughout the
world of electrical vortices are sacred mountains. In his
marvelous book *Mountain Dialogues*, author Frank Waters defines sacred mountains as "repositories of psychic
energy upon which mankind draws for its life and development. We may, I suppose, loosely regard them as psychic power plants analogous to our physical power
plants." Waters also points out that sacred mountains
"serve as focal points or distribution centers located on
all continents throughout the planet."

Most sacred mountains are intense electrical power-
houses that have been revered by indigenous cultures. It
is still common for annual or even more frequent "pilgrimages" to the summits to be conducted. As a rule,
these sacred journeys are for ceremonial purposes, designed to renew the faith of the people or to usher in a
new year or religious cycle. As journeys for spiritual reasons are conducted, participants can experience inspiring
and renewing energies that can reestablish faith and hope.
There might also be healings, particularly with those individuals whose health problems may be psychological
or of a magnetic-type illness, for the surge in electrical
life power could "correct" the problem.

Forty miles north of my home in Sedona, Arizona, on
the outskirts of Flagstaff, stand the wonderfully majestic
San Francisco Peaks. Dominating the lava-covered Co-

conino Plateau, the "Peaks," as they are called locally, are 12,670-foot-high slopes and multiple summits which are sacred to both the Hopi and the Navajo Indian tribes. Sculptured by fire and ice, the Peaks are like sentinels standing mute over millions of acres of ponderosa pine and aspen. The three summits, named Humphreys, Agassiz, and Fremont by nonnatives, are dotted with various shrines put there by the native people, primarily the Hopi, at different times throughout their ceremonial year for several purposes. This has been going on for hundreds of years.

Perhaps the most noteworthy information about the Peaks is that, according to Hopi tradition, they are the home of the kachinas. Kachinas, or Cloud People, are the nature gods and goddesses of the Hopi who bring rain, help crops to grow, discipline the children, and embody the Sun and all the forces of Nature. Each year on the occasion of the *Niman* Ceremony, the kachinas leave the Peaks to interact with the Hopi people in their ceremonies and in other areas of their lives from late December through the following July. In spite of the ski lodges that have been built on the slopes of the Peaks, and the U.S. government's claim of ownership, the San Francisco Peaks are still sacred ground to the native people.

Some electrical vortices are not mountains per se, but volcanic life-forms. Two such places that come to mind are Mount Shasta in northern California and Mount Kilauea, the currently erupting volcano in Hawaii. Aside from being electrical vortices and having the same effects that any electrical vortex would have on humans, both of these sites have something else in common. These and many other sacred mountains have *spirits* associated with them that are usually considered to be the life force of the mountain itself personified. The "spirit presences" associated with Mount Shasta and explanations put forth to explain them cover quite a broad range of phenomena.

Mount Shasta is an impressive sight. A part of the electrical Cascade Range, Shasta is located in the northern extremity of the California Sierra Nevadas. The cone of an extinct volcano, so it is said, Shasta has been worn away by the activity of ages of wind and ice. I question this peak being considered extinct, for it *could* actually erupt due to a sulfurous furole that lies below the extreme summit and one or two others on its northern slope, which I found out about as a result of my research for my previous book, *The Earth Changes Survival Handbook*.

Some of the strange tales surrounding Mount Shasta involve the sighting of "weird people" who come, apparently, out of the forest. These people seem to go to great lengths, according to those who have sighted them, to not be accosted or even seen by passersby. Reports of sightings become more unusual when you consider that witnesses say that these strangers wear uniquely mysterious headdresses and clothing which some believe are like those worn in ancient Lemurian times. They also have large heads, especially the foreheads, and are graceful and agile in body. A contradiction arises concerning their shyness, however, when some reports have them paying for goods purchased in local stores with gold nuggets! Lemurians? Members of a hippie cult left over from the sixties? Spirit beings? Extraterrestrials? Who can say?

UFO sightings are also common at Shasta. Accounts persist of automobiles not functioning properly, apparently due to *electrical* problems, as do sightings of strange flying objects, lights, and even "chants" made by human voices. I think that electrical problems with cars or any vehicles may be explained by the surge of electrical current emanating from the vortex itself. But the other stories would certainly require much more research than this writing permits. For the interested reader, there is a book devoted solely to the subject of Mount Shasta and its strange happenings entitled *Lemuria: The Lost Continent of the Pacific, the Mystery People of Mt. Shasta*, by Walter S. Cerve, published by the Rosicrucians.

An account of the spiritual prowess of Mount Shasta has been reported by Robert and Earlyne Chaney, the founders of Astara, in Upland, California, in their book *Secrets from Mt. Shasta*. Described as an "initiation by fire," the Chaneys tell of being "drawn" to the mountain by "unseen teachers" for an initiation that took the form of a "blinding flash over a certain rock." I find it interesting that the words used to describe their experience are: "blinding flash," "explosion," "flashes of lightning," and "blazing star of light," all of which are terms easily associated with our earlier description of electrical Life Energy.

Located on the Pacific Island of Hawaii, Kilauea is an active volcano and refers to an electrical vortex. The most distinguishing legend of this vortex is its indwelling spirit goddess, Pele. Pele has not always been associated with Kilauea. More ancient accounts have her creating salt lakes, rock formations, and craters on the islands of Maui, Kauai, Oahu, and Molokai. The fire goddess has finally settled, for now, on the big island at Kilauea, where she continues her building of new land. Reverence for Pele is ancient. Seen as a woman, Pele appears just before and during an eruption. A temperamental spirit, Pele's wrath is incurred when she is shown disrespect. The stomping of her feet causes the very ground to tremble. Descriptions of Pele are quite specific. They include "priestesses" who accompany her, who "wore robes whose sleeves and hems had been burnt ragged by fire, and carried a wand or digging stick, in imitation of the *Paoa* staff that Pele had used when She . . . first dug the volcanic craters." Many have seen Pele. In fact, although I had not been to Hawaii at the time, I saw her appear quite unexpectedly while I was viewing a video of a Kilauea eruption. Sadly, Christianity discouraged worship of the fire goddess, but the stories and beliefs persist, and Pele has been called upon many times to protect life and property from the advance of the hot lava flows from the powerful eruptions.

I have had my own enlightening personal experience with a sacred mountain. On a working/pleasure trip to Alaska in 1985, my husband, Scott, and I were instructed by Albion (my Spirit Teacher) to make a "pilgrimage" to Denali. Denali, better known as Mount McKinley, is touted as the second tallest mountain in the world. Known to the indigenous peoples as Denali, "The Great One," this 20,320-foot peak is truly a magnificent reservoir of pure electrical power that constitutes an electrical vortex.

For some time, Scott and I had been giving serious thought to relocating to Alaska to live for a couple of years, to experience this powerful part of the Earth's body. Our study of natural Earth energies, so strong in Alaska, could be furthered by living there in such a unique environment. We were told to "go to the mountain" on a sort of "vision quest" and to listen for direction or advice from Denali regarding our decision about a move.

Upon our arrival at the sacred mountain, we followed our instincts to give our offering of a medicine bundle of sage and some other herbs and minerals and then to sit quietly in a receptive frame of mind. Before long, I became aware of a thought passing through my mind: If I could hear the "voice" of the mountain as a sound, what would it sound like? I listened intently. The first sound that came to mind was faint, but it grew louder after a few moments. It was like a foghorn that can be heard on a misty night on Cape Cod, and sounded about every ten seconds or so. Although I allowed the sound to fade from my mind, I could tune into it, at will, afterward, and can still hear it clearly today. After allowing Denali's voice to fade, I "felt" the mountain "speak" to me, asking in a loud voice inside my head: "Why are you here? What do you want?" I was a bit startled and, as everyone else must feel, wondered if it was only my imagination. I remembered my own words in teaching basic psychic development and knew that the imagination is the fundamental tool of psychic sensitivity. So I relaxed and responded to the question with the thought of our possible move to Alaska and our reasons. After a few moments, when I had finished and quieted my mind once again, I received a reply: "You are not strong enough, physically, for this land." I knew the mountain had spoken, and I knew, intuitively, that its words were correct. If I wanted to live in Alaska, I would have to make every effort to strengthen myself and my physical body.

Albion gave me a definition of an electrical vortex that

cleared up many questions in my mind about the purposes served by sacred mountains to the health of the
body of the Earth. "Sacred mountains, and all electrical
vortices, are *distributors of Life Force* throughout the
Earth's form." That definition helped me to understand
that such vortices act as a sort of "relay system" for life
power from one place to another, not unlike the cardio-
vascular system in the human body. Aside from the general definition of a vortex found on the actual body of the
Earth, there are two additional types of vortices whose
purposes and functions differ from those that we have
discussed so far. These are "synthesizers" and "beacons."

Synthesizer Vortices

Synthesizers are a type of atmospheric vortex and are
strategically located above certain areas of the Earth.
There are only sixteen of them. Synthesizers act in two
ways: They give and sustain the Earth's "balance," and
they are the source and, therefore, the originating points
of weather fronts. Also, the role of a synthesizer as a
"polarizing agent" is evidenced in the Earth's poles,
both north and south. The poles are necessary vortices
of electromagnetic Life Energy whose presence generates a sort of balancing effect. The equator of the planet
is another synthesizer that unites the hemispheres and
keeps them in balance. Others are weather synthesizers,
like the "Vancouver Vortex," which takes its name from
its location in the general area of Vancouver, British Columbia. Such a vortex generates what will become high-
and low-pressure systems that pass over the continent,
primarily the United States, resulting in weather activity
for one to two weeks, as a rule. Still others are located
in the Baja area of extreme southern California, the Ber-
muda area, near the West Indies, the Red Sea area, and
the upper midcentral area of Canada. When this particular synthesizer is operating at full force, the United

States gets an icy blast of cold air sometimes called the "Arctic Express."

Beacon Vortices

Beacon vortices are truly unique in their function in regards to the livingness of the planet. These powerful sites are the fewest in number. There are fewer than twenty-five worldwide. A beacon vortex is the site of a special type of ley terminal, a place where the incoming energies of a major ley line system join together into a complex conjunction point of electric, magnetic, or electromagnetic energy. The vortex itself "shoots" the energy into space, where it connects with other planets in the Solar System, the Sun, or the Moon, galaxies and stars. It is through these kinds of vortices that the Earth is not only linked to other bodies, but they also act as "receiving points" through which other planetary and luminary energies are received into our planet's aura and body. This is what makes astrology work, for example, by the influencing forces that gain access to the Earth and her life-forms through these beacon vortices.

A recent interview with the well-known Cherokee medicine chief Harley Swiftdeer shed a great deal of light upon my understanding of "beacon" vortices. When discussing Cherokee Sacred Sites, Harley mentioned Lookout Mountain, now known as Stone Mountain, on the outskirts of Atlanta, Georgia. "Lookout Mountain was, and still is, a ceremonial site to my people. It is a 'connecting' place . . . one that connects human consciousness to the *Star Nation* (italics mine) . . . to the Pleiades, in particular." When I heard those words I immediately flashed on the beacon vortices, and many things fell into place in my mind. I thought about the beacons, for example, as being sites that possess "celestial" leys or lines that connect the Earth to other bodies in outer space. Such a link was surely what Swiftdeer was implying. I realized that, like the Skidi Pawnee people of Nebraska, he was saying that the Indians believed, and still do, in the reality of the great Star Nation, their intelligence, and their being a source of tremendous power. I also thought about the curious fact that there are so many reported UFO sightings and related phenomena at the beacon vortices I know of.

Native Americans, and other even more ancient cultures, were known to experience a mental and spiritual connection to the stars. The following is an excerpt from an article I wrote entitled "Skywalkers" that discusses this fact and its role in the development and practices of arcane shamans.

The experience required for the living to enter into the supernatural, celestial worlds calls for unusually precise knowledge and skills. It could be said it is a "calling," the business of specialists. Such specialists are shamans. Many of their visions, ceremonies, and other mystical practices are designed to carry them to the sky. Being connected to the Earth Mother is surely considered desirable by all the native peoples. But, having access to the heavens is of equal value and importance. Visions obtained by the shamans in their contact with the Sky Gods is, to them, an echo of Cosmic Order. The shaman's interaction with the sky helps them—and us—to understand the sky's role in the human consciousness and in human life. In short, to the shaman, intimacy with the stars and other celestial bodies is a must.

In order to gain a clearer understanding of celestial shamanic practices, I feel we need to go far back into time, prior to the rituals of the Native Americans, to the ancient religions of China. The Chinese have long been accurate skywatchers and have recorded celestial events, some of which comprise the only available data and observations of supernovas, comets, eclipses and the like that occurred in the dim past. The supernova in Taurus in 1054 A.D. is a classic example of an event that left us with remnants of the death of a great star now known to modern astronomers as the Crab Nebula.

This nebula, subsequently, became the first pulsar—a rapidly spinning star core—to be discovered.

Religion in ancient China was filled with and preserved many practices that can be considered "shamanic" in nature. Medieval Chinese in the T'ang Dynasty believed that ascent into the heavens was possible through specific use of the mind. Meditative techniques were employed by which priests could roam the skies. It is said that in their mind's eye they would concentrate on selected constellations or stellar patterns and, in doing so, muster the power to climb to the sky. It is believed that there were many paths into the sky via a planet, a constellation, perhaps even through a comet or some other entity or celestial form such as the sky-bridge we call the Milky Way. It is also known that all of the native tribes on the North American Continent, for example, attached considerable significance to the star-bridge, calling it the Gateway to the Spirit World, the Rainbow Bridge, and other names that imply its sacredness. Entering into the sky, for all mystics in the East and West, was and is, no doubt, a truly transcendental experience. However it was accomplished, the goal was and is the same—to enter into the center of the Cosmos, into the sacred realms of Time-Space. Conscious unity of this sort is said to be far beyond the senses and reason whenever it is achieved.

I believe that the beacon vortices, located worldwide, were unique places where man and stars could and did meet in order to engage in a powerful celestial dance of life and meaning.

Bell Rock, one of the electrical vortex sites in Sedona, is another such beacon. It is interesting to note that in these particular areas the effect of the energy experienced is usually quite intense on human consciousness. It can result in a tremendous uplifting of the soul consciousness, and there are frequent reports of astral travel and "out of the body" incidents occurring spontaneously. As with Stone Mountain, UFO sightings and experiences are also a rather common report associated with Bell Rock. Other beacon sites are Mount Sinai in Israel, Devil's Tower in Wyoming, and the Glastonbury Tor in England. Still others are pointed out in the listing of Sacred Sites and vortices in remaining chapters.

If the electrical vortices disperse the life force that enlivens the Earth's physical body, then there must be some vehicle by which or through which the prana travels from one point to another. There is. This system is made up of a complex network of *leys* that are located throughout the planetary body, including her aura.

Ley Lines in the Living Earth

The theory of *ley lines* dates far back into antiquity, perhaps originating with the Chinese, who called them "dragon lines." In more recent times, we must credit the most thorough investigation of these energy circuits to an Englishman, Alfred Watkins. An enthusiastic photographer, Watkins, at the age of sixty-five, while riding across the green hills of his homeland, perceived in a flash the existence of the ley system. Watkins believed that he had rediscovered "the key plan of a long lost fact." In his now republished book, *The Old Straight Track*, Watkins tells his story of discovery and develops his theory. Watkins recounts how he first recognized that ancient travelers had "marked" their routes with crude pegs. Looking out over the landscape during an afternoon horse ride, he saw the network of leys, which he described as "standing out like glowing wires all over the surface of the country, intersecting at the sites of churches, old stones, and other spots of traditional sanctity." By pointing out the presence of ceremonial buildings and other man-placed objects at "traditional spots of sanctity," he had, no doubt, happened across an integral truth about the Ancients' knowledge of Earth energy and its path through the Earth's body.

A ley line is like a hollow wire through which energy is conducted. Because these lines of force are quite numerous, they *cross* or *intersect* at various points on the planet. I call such intersections *conjunction points* and/or *ley terminals*, are places where the current, either electric, magnetic, or electromagnetic, is especially strong. In some places these terminal points correspond to actual vortex locations, but more often they constitute minivortices that are the sites of intense energy.

A good friend and fellow teacher and author, William Bloom of London, in his booklet *Ley Lines and Ecology: An Introduction*, writes: "Ley lines, then, form the matrix of energy which is the *dynamic physical principle* of the geological body of Earth. Ley lines are the essential structure of the etheric body of the Earth Spirit." Bloom goes on to say that "these lines vary from five miles to approximately two thousand miles; they are straight but not dead straight and may undulate gently." I agree, for the most part, although I think that leys can be much longer than the approximated two thousand miles Bloom proposes. Some reach all the way around the planet.

Electrical vortices are connected by electric ley lines, transporting Earth electricity from one vortex point to another. There are also magnetic leys that connect and conduct magnetic energy, and the same is true for electromagnetic vortices. When leys conducting one type of Earth energy intersect with leys conducting another type or charge, the energies involved are enhanced, resulting in some "terminals" being locations of two or more forces. These places are particularly intense multienergy sites having the accompanying effects inherent in each of the life energies present. Intersections where leys of the *same* type of Life Energy cross each other are where actual vortices are to be found.

An intriguing comment concerning ley lines was brought out in Colin Wilson's monumental work entitled *Mysteries*. Wilson quotes his sources as suggesting that on the sites of ley lines there can be various manifestations of psychic-type phenomena ranging from healings, poltergeist activity, and ghosts, to physical/emotional reactions of dizziness, disorientation, and ecstasy. There is also an old English belief that if one slept on a ley line, the dreams would be enhanced, some even foretelling the future.

There is one other term to be aware of: the *grid*. I define it as a highly charged location that is *not* coagulated into an actual *vortex*. A grid, as a rule, covers a larger geographical location, with its energy equally spread out over that given area. Furthermore, a grid can be the result of ley terminals or major underground sources of energy such as aquifers or liquid lava flows. Large river areas such as the Ganges and the Nile or Amazon will often be considered grids. Other examples of grids include the magnetic Florida Everglades, the electric Sahara, Sonoran, and other large deserts, and the electromagnetic island of Maui in Hawaii.

Magnetic Vortices

Let us now turn our attention to *magnetic* vortices, which can also be found worldwide. Because magnetism is the opposite of electricity, magnetic vortices calm the body, mind, and emotions. Magnetic vortices are most famous for their healing powers, and many of them are the sacred waters of the world, usually in the form of healing wells, springs, and sometimes entire rivers or lakes. Lourdes, in France, is a prime example of an aquatic healing site and magnetic vortex. The Ganges River in India is a magnetic grid.

It is believed that in ancient Britain there were actually water cults that may have originated some five thousand years ago. These were people who valued water as sacred. They performed ceremonies and left gifts to the water spirits as their religious practice. Some researchers believe that there is ample evidence to support the theory that avenues of stone, often accompanying megalithic circle sites, usually lead from a source of water. An example would be Stonehenge, whose water source is the nearby Avon River. To date, there are some two-hundred-plus ancient and holy wells that have survived and are being used in the British Isles. Drinking water from a sacred well or spring has been known to result in cures of all kinds, with some wells being said to treat specific ailments of certain parts of the body.

Aside from their healing qualities, magnetic vortices also have the effect of quieting the body and mind to make meditation and prayer more effective. Memory is more easily accessed at a magnetic vortex. Many people have reported having past life recall at such sites. Visions and dreams are also more intense and likely to occur at magnetic power spots. I have known Albion to advise individuals to go to a magnetic vortex when they were in need of complete rest and relaxation, relying on the vortex to help them get what they needed.

Magnetic vortices stimulate the flow of creative energy and lend themselves well to creative people. If intuition is *the* source of creativity, then magnetic vortices are excellent places for intuition to intensify. For this reason, magnetic vortices serve as perfect locations for vision quests if people are seeking inner guidance. Magnetic vortices, worldwide, include: the Chalice Well in Glastonbury, England; Lourdes in France; the sacred lake at Karnak Temple in Egypt; and Lake Titicaca on the border of Peru and Bolivia. Examples of *magnetic grids* include: the Florida Everglades, the Okefenoke Swamp, and Idaho Springs in the state of Colorado, in the United States; the Island of Bimini; and the city of Venice in Italy.

Caves are another type of magnetic vortex, although not every cave qualifies as an actual vortex. The Earth itself is a gigantic magnet, and much of the body of the Earth is magnetic in nature. Caves have often been the site of ceremony, as evidenced by petroglyphs that have been discovered at such places. Some of the caves are not located underground and are found in highly electrical areas like the southwestern deserts of North America. Caves that are magnetic vortices or grids include the Pyrennean and Dardogne Caves in St. Girons in France; the Drach Caves in Spain; Adjanta, a magnetic grid in the western part of India; and the famed Mammoth Caves in the state of Kentucky in America.

Magnetic Synthesizer Vortices

The Earth's atmosphere is particularly susceptible to forming temporary magnetic vortices called synthesizers. The purpose of these electromagnetic weather vortices/synthesizers is to trigger and transport vast amounts of water that magnetize the Earth's body and replenish her water supplies. Cyclones, waterspouts, hurricanes, and typhoons are manifestations of magnetic power, as are tornadoes spawned by severe thunderstorm and low-pressure activity. This represents a tremendous release of magnetic atmospheric potential energy. As most of these tropical storms occur over tropical-like or magnetic areas, they are the Earth's way of replenishing her supply of magnetism, just as lightning, volcanoes, and solar rays are the way she receives and replenishes her electrical supply. Both are necessary components for life.

Magnetism and Fairy Lore

During the past few years I have pursued an interest in the Angelic Kingdom and its relationship to the Earth, as well as to human beings. In my research of the so-called *nature spirits*, I have discovered that many cultures have tales about the "devas," especially in Europe and the British Isles.

Janet and Colin Bord's book *The Secret Country* is a wealth of information concerning, among other geomantic information, the fairy lore of Great Britain. As the authors say, "The study of fairy lore is complex: each writer on the subject often favours a different explanation to cover the whole range of traditions." It is curious that there are numerous fairy folk legends that link many of the megalithic sites, both circles and single standing stones, to the appearance and activity of various types of nature spirits. These magnetic vortices, called "fairy rings," have truly captured my interest. Janet and Colin Bord are convinced that there is a connection between the fairy rings and certain Earth currents, which I call magnetism, and/or ley lines. Many of the places where folklore originates are intense magnetic vortex areas. We know that such energy can awaken psychic faculties. It can also cause our consciousness to move inward, sometimes into a deep sleep or trancelike altered state. In such states, time can become distorted, seeming to some to slow down and to others to speed up. Remember Washington Irving's Rip Van Winkle, who fell asleep for twenty years? It is interesting that in many of the accounts of human encounters with fairy-folk, all or part of my theory holds true. An example is given in *The Secret Country*: "The stories of mortals joining fairies in their dances and losing awareness of Earth-time, emerging apparently only minutes later to find years elapsed, may simply be indications of the power of the Earth current, its ability to overwhelm the senses of the inexperienced, to cause temporal and spatial dislocation." While I have not interviewed anyone who has had such an experience, I am aware of the persistent belief in nature spirits and their connection to the Earth. The *fairy rings*, which are purported to be the site of the little peoples' emergence and return into the Earth, are sites of peculiar "magnetic" behavior. I've often wondered if "fairy rings," which are commonly seen in the fields of Britain and France, are indeed a type of minor magnetic vortex. Several peculiar attributes are noted about them, such as a lack of grass growth, reminiscent of the same phenomenon reported at the "Devil's Footprints" in North Carolina. It is also in a magnetic area and has the same lore as Europe's fairy rings. For now, I leave these thoughts with the reader and hold any conclusions for further research on the subject.

Electromagnetic Vortices

Next, let us consider electromagnetic vortices. Although not as plentiful as magnetic vortices or grids, they exist worldwide as well. The most distinguishing feature of an electromagnetic vortex is its ability to create a balance between electricity and magnetism in all life-forms. We know that vortex energy affects all the four major levels of man, namely the physical, emotional, mental, and spiritual. An electromagnetic vortex will most influence whatever aspect of the individual is out of balance. For example, if the physical health is the cause of the imbalance, a healing could result. If the emotions are imbalanced, causing depression or any number of other problems, the electromagnetic vortex may help to bring things into a clearer perspective so the person can better deal with his feelings.

We must keep in mind that *balance* is the key here. In places that are naturally electromagnetic but have had that harmony disturbed, the result is an intense energy distortion. These places can have an adverse effect on humans or other life-forms, causing an imbalance on some level of body and/or consciousness. The level most likely to be affected would be the one that is the weakest and most vulnerable. This sort of possible problem would be particularly applicable to those who live full-time in such an area. Electromagnetic locations may become imbalanced due to a city being founded and, over time, growing into a huge metropolis. This would add so much electricity to the area that the natural magnetism would simply be overcome. People in these places would suffer, after a period of time, from a diminishing sensitivity and perception. The pace of life in the area could become extremely hectic, and it's probable that the crime rate would rise.

Flooding can create a temporary imbalance of an electromagnetic vortex or grid, as can changes in climatic trends that result in an increase of rainfall or other forms of precipitation over a period of time. Albion has talked about the water being the source of the magnetism, while the intense movement of it generates the electricity. Most waterfalls are in electromagnetic terrains, while the waterfall itself is the actual vortex. Examples of electromagnetic vortices and grids are Yellowstone Falls, Angel Falls, and Niagara Falls.

The islands of Maui and Kauai of Hawaii are electromagnetic grids, and each has several vortices. Jamaica is an electromagnetic island. The entire territory of Alaska is an electromagnetic grid, as are the general Pacific Northwest, and the Blue Ridge, Smoky, and Rocky Mountain ranges. Blowing Rock and Caesar's Head in the Smokies are electromagnetic vortices. These types of vortices and grids are of special benefit to people who feel a need for restoration of balance and harmony in their lives. They would also be ideal locations for healing and therapy centers and spiritual retreats.

Making Use of Vortices

The concept that the Earth is alive becomes astonishingly apparent when we apply the Life Energy System to it. With the simple guidelines the system provides, we can go to any place on the Earth and know, at least generally, which of the three Life Energies are present and what basic effect those powers can have on our bodies and consciousness.

Making use of vortices and Sacred Sites is a step toward better Earth awareness, and we do have examples to follow. Most Sacred Sites were used for ceremony by the various tribes of any given region. Depending on the particular practices of any given tribe, ceremonies involved a gathering of the people who performed rituals designed to communicate with the Great Spirit and with the intelligent consciousness of the members of the other Kingdoms of Life . . . rocks, wind, water, animals, and plants. It was the recognition of man's relationship with all life-forms that set the standard of "equality" by which all lived. John Redtail Freesoul, in his book *Breath of the Invisible*, explains the nature and value of Native

American ceremony and the importance of symbols as embodying the Forces of Nature itself:

"Symbols and ceremony can be blueprints for these tools of *perceptions* (italics mine) and point us to the reality behind them. They can also become vehicles of travel to the destination of inner realization and outer awareness. Our knowledge, awareness, and realization increase through conscious and willful communication with our inner self, with other forms in nature, and with the spirit world. In this way our consciousness expands, preparing us to commune with Source, the Great Spirit. All is connected. Each union leads to another. Knowledge without awareness and realization does not yield wisdom and is unbalanced."

In the life of the Native American, some ceremonies were held at the solstices and equinoxes to mark the seasons. These were times of planting, harvesting, of hunting for food, and times when the spirit powers were most intense. Ceremonies of this sort were done not only to celebrate, but also for the purpose of "initiating" certain tribal members into higher levels of consciousness and/or spiritual positions within the tribe or clan. Ceremony was also a vehicle for personal growth. One of the most powerful ceremonies I know is native to the Plains Indians and is referred to as the "Sweat." This strenuous rite is for the purpose of personal cleansing and purification and was performed, as a rule, prior to a vision quest, a marriage ceremony, after a death, or for physical healing.

Vision Quest

Another use of vortices and Sacred Sites is the vision quest. The vision quest is best described as a rite of passage, a re-creation of the act of dying and being reborn. Usually conducted on a mountaintop, in a secluded woodland area, near a waterfall, or some other area chosen for its beauty, power, and privacy, the vision quest was a time when the individual used the Earth Mother and forces of Nature to facilitate a "vision" of one's personal future. Sometimes the images would unfold in dreams, atmospheric omens, through the appearance of one's totem, the inner voice, or through "spirit talk" that results in altered states of consciousness. Perhaps no other ceremony depended so greatly on the "connection" man had with the Earth.

Sacred Sites

Sacred Sites were often places where wheel-like structures were built, primarily by the people of the American Great Plains. The wheels are one of the few distinguishing features of these prehistoric people, namely the Crow, Cheyenne, Comanche, Sioux, Kiowa, Blackfoot, and Pawnee. Throughout the Plains are remnants of thousands of stone circles that range from six to eighteen feet in diameter, which give evidence of these human settlements. The small circles have been dubbed "tepee rings" and are believed to have held down the tepee coverings. In addition to the small rings, larger stone circles and patterns were often found. Some were long, low stone walls and alignments, while others were stone effigies. The most intriguing of all the wheel-like structures are the "medicine wheels," named for their association with sacred spirits and natural forces. The wheels that have been discovered are a variety of sizes and designs, usually an avenue of stones leading out from a central rock cairn, reminiscent of the spoke of a wheel. The most accepted theory on the purpose of the medicine wheels is that they served a calendrical as well as a ceremonial purpose.

Sacred Site Preservation and Use

Much time has passed and many changes have occurred since Native Americans discovered and/or established their special places of worship and ceremony. Time and the advent of the white civilization have taken their toll, especially on the physical side of many Sacred Sites. As with some of the sites in, for example, the British Isles and the European continent, stones of the medicine wheels have been removed or plowed under, cairns and other special rocks have been hidden, perhaps mercifully, from view and understanding. Many of the people who honored and used certain sites for communication with their nature deities have disappeared from the human family, taking with them the secrets and wisdom they held so dear. Still other sacred places are now on privately owned land. As a result, there is mounting concern among native and non-native people throughout the country for the accessibility and preservation of both ancient and current Sacred Sites. I encountered evidence of this concern in my own quest for the locations of the sacred areas for this book. Time after time, the people with whom I spoke expressed concern over the sites being revealed for fear of their being damaged, physically, by an influx of visitors. They're also concerned that the sites will be "misused" and that their power will be drained. Others felt that it is important, especially now, for people to know the whereabouts of the Sacred Sites so that they can learn of their importance and the need to protect them.

In the course of my interviews for this book, I encountered many individuals whose concern for the recognition and preservation of Sacred Sites in the United States and other lands has become a spiritual path unto itself. One such person is Tek Nickerson, the Founder of SHARE, INC. (the Native American Clothing Bank), and the recently formed Sacred Sites Conservancy. Nickerson's concerns are, quite simply, "to acquire and protect Sacred Sites from abusive activities for the equitable access of all spiritual truthseekers." The Sacred Sites

Conservancy, fashioned after the nationally known organization the Nature Conservancy, seeks public participation and tax-deductible donations to help return such lands to sacred use, in full cooperation with the native people. ''Sacred Sites must be protected as soon as possible, to prevent or reverse their encroachment upon by picnickers, skiers (San Francisco Peaks, Arizona), and bathers (Hot Springs, South Dakota).''

One site that has triggered Nickerson's and others' involvement is Bear Butte in South Dakota. The following is part of a letter I received from Nickerson, showing the plight of one place that is, sadly, the same that threatens other Sacred Sites and vortex areas.

''Near the western central border of South Dakota sits the legendary Mato Paha, or Bear Butte. On the periphery of Paha Sapa, or Black Hills, Bear Butte lies within the original treaty territory of the Lakota Sioux. It is here that Sweet Medicine, prophet of the Northern Cheyenne, received Four Commandments for his people, just as Moses received Ten Commandments for his people upon Mount Sinai. For as long as people have crossed these plains, Bear Butte drew and continues to draw people to it, not only by its solitary stark appearance breaking the horizon, but by its unique and powerful spiritual energy. As Mecca is to the Moslems, Bear Butte is to the Northern Plains Indians, and is no less sacred by any sense of the word. For this reason every summer, many traditional Plains Indians pray and vision quest upon Bear Butte's flanks and crest, as they have done for over 4,000 years.

In the 1960s, the state of South Dakota purchased 1,600 acres, or nearly half of Bear Butte, for a state park. Since then, tourists have climbed Bear Butte with little regard for the sanctity of the place, picnicking and trashing the crest and trails with beer cans and debris. Picture tourists chopping up the altar at Saint Peter's Basilica for a campfire, roasting hotdogs, swilling beer, and trashing the marble floor with gooey wrappers, and you can begin to imagine the indignity felt by a proud people who hold Bear Butte no less sacred.

While the Lakota hold legal claim to Bear Butte under the treaty of 1868, they have not the funds for a successful legal contest. The Lakota cannot purchase the land, because that would weaken their claim to title. Meanwhile, the Northern Cheyenne have been acquiring parcels within surrounding Bear Butte, in order to protect it from further abuse. Recent events indicate that abuses are occurring faster than the Northern Cheyenne can afford to acquire property.

Of particular concern is the growing popularity of the annual summer motorcycle rally, sponsored by the nearby town of Sturgis, South Dakota. The 1988 event drew 80,000–100,000 motorcyclists, or ''hogs'' as they prefer to be called. For the small town of 5,000, this event plays a major role to strengthen an economic base weakened by drought and ranch failures. Many landowners are turning their ranches into campgrounds, some temporarily for the rally, and some more permanently. One such ranch is located at the base of Bear Butte, near a sacred healing spring. This ranch hosted up to 500 ''hogs'' in 1988, complete with video arcade and a beer permit.

A few days before the start of the 1988 rally, a family of mixed Native American heritage camped at this ranch to check out what was happening. The grandfather spirits of Bear Butte presented these visitors with a message and urgent request: ''Tell the campground operators that this behavior is inappropriate for this place, and set up an organization that will protect Bear Butte's dignity for all prayerful people to seek equitably.'' The message was given to the campground owners, but it was ignored.

In light of this kind of tragedy, we can understand the reluctance of the Native American people to reveal the locations of Sacred Sites. We can also understand the frustration that continues to be experienced by Indian people throughout the country due to so many of their sacred lands being vandalized and disrespected or simply no longer being accessible because they are on what is now private land.

While on a working trip to Omaha, Nebraska, in 1987, my husband and I were informed of the location of a Sacred Site, actually an entire village site, of the Skidi Pawnee people, some thirty-five miles outside the city. I was particularly thrilled with this information, because for some time I had been making a special study of the Skidi. As an amateur astronomer, I found these now extinct people of special interest because of their unique cosmology and their belief that they came to Earth from the stars. This belief system made them some of the earliest astronomers on the continent and set them aside from all other native peoples.

It turned out that the site was on private land, currently owned by a retired physician and his wife. Our friend in Omaha, Tom Workman, obtained permission for us to visit the area for the purpose of conducting a pipe and Earth healing ceremony. Called Pahuk, which translates to mean Pumpkin Vine Village, the area was once the location of one of the four major villages of the Pawnee Federation. It was also a ceremonial area, as well as the spot where the so-called Animal Lodge could only be entered via the dream state. The animals, according to the Skidi, were the teachers of men.

Upon entering the area where Pahuk once existed, I felt a sense of the power of the ceremonials that had taken place so long ago. The air was crisp and the river flowed ever so silently in the background, its presence making itself felt in the humid environment. It was as if I could still participate in the prayers and smell the smoke of the villages now gone from this sacred place. Being there was a truly uplifting experience and one that served to connect me with the dreams and lives of the Skidi people.

Sacred Site Etiquette

Although there are no set rules to follow when approaching or experiencing a Sacred Site, I have, over the years, learned many techniques that are designed for the purpose of helping the Seeker to succeed in creating a well-balanced relationship with such places. In later chapters we'll get to specific ceremonies that can be performed at Sacred Sites, but here are some important thoughts to consider before you begin your journey.

Preparation for going to a sacred area is very practical. The experience you have can be greatly diminished if you feel angry or otherwise emotionally distressed. Centering yourself as best as possible prior to your visit is, therefore, quite helpful.

When you set out to visit a particular vortex site for the energy it embodies, this constitutes a pilgrimage, a journey with special spiritual intent. Great distances can be involved to reach such a place, and you may encounter and have to overcome any number of personal obstacles. So it is very important that the journey itself be as successful as possible. Learning all you can about the place is advisable, but it is also necessary to regulate your own energy. Fasting, getting proper rest, having proper attire for prevailing weather conditions, as well as making sure that the site you are seeking is not on private property, are some ways to accomplish this. If it is on private property, you must gain permission for your visit from the proper authorities. I am including, at the end of this chapter, a list you may wish to carry with you as a reminder of the proper and necessary behavior one must exhibit at a Sacred Site or natural vortex.

Sacred Sites and vortices are usually protected by angels and/or other spirits. Recognition of these entities is necessary so that your personal energy is of no threat. When you visit such areas you bring along the "vibrations" of who and what you are, where you have been, and with whom you have been associated. Remember that the guardian spirits are extremely sensitive to your presence. Enlisting their cooperation and openness to your energy can mean the difference between having a positive or negative experience. Announce your presence and your reasons for being there, either aloud or silently, to establish a psychic dialogue between yourself and the spirits present. Asking for permission to partake of the powers is a good idea as well. I must say that there have been occasions when I have sensed that the time was not appropriate or for some other reason I should not stay at a particular site. Whenever such a feeling occurs, I feel it must be honored and I return at another time. Frequently visited places often get depleted in energy, and it would not be appropriate to put a further drain on the vortex. Time for a rebuilding of the power is needed in this case, so again, I would choose to return at a later time. Also, it is always proper to carry an offering to the spirits of a Sacred Site. Offerings may be herbs such as sage, tobacco, or one that is of special spiritual significance to you. Other gifts can be a few of your hairs, a small crystal or other mineral, or any object that "feels right." Keep in mind that the offering will be left behind, so it should not deface the site or in any way be distracting to other visitors.

Once you have spoken to the resident guardians, placed your offering, and feel good about staying for a while, it is appropriate to sit quietly for prayer and/or meditation. With the exception of water from holy wells, it is not acceptable to take stones or plants away from the site.

When your visit comes to a close, a prayer for healing of the sacred spot is a good idea. You can be certain that these places have a "mind" of their own, and that what is in your heart is sensed. The most important thing to keep in mind is the livingness of the Earth. Going to a sacred place requires that one go in a sacred way. This will assure a rewarding and beneficial experience with the spirits and the energies of the location and a greater openness between the two.

Let us now begin our journey to the five countries selected to demonstrate the Life Energy System. These lands are energy-rich, no doubt the main reason for their sacred histories, their effect on human evolution, and their intense spiritual attributes.

POINTS TO BE REMEMBERED
REGARDING SACRED SITES AND VORTICES

1. Gain permission if the site is on private land.
2. Do not use or carry vehicles into areas where there is no road access, to eliminate damage to the terrain.
3. Self-cleansing is imperative before visiting a Sacred Site. This can take the form of bathing, physically, a sweat ceremony for cleansing other levels of yourself, making peace in any area of your life where there is disharmony, and/or spending time in prayer for purification.
4. Go alone or in small groups.
5. When speaking of the site to others, be selective. Likewise, be informative as to the need to maintain the area.
6. Never go to a power spot when in a negative frame of mind.
7. Carry an offering.
8. Honor and address the spirit keepers and/or guardians of the place.
9. Leave no trash behind.
10. Be careful not to create a fire hazard with pipe smoking, smudge, or other use of flammable substances.
11. Leave nothing behind that would deface the area even if it is a personal offering. You may bury it as long as it does not require displacing large amounts of soil or any amount of plant life or animal habitats.
12. As a rule, the energy at a Sacred Site is most potent at sunrise or sunset, and you may wish to plan your pilgrimage accordingly.
13. Conduct personal ceremonies in quiet and with respect.
14. Talk to Nature.
15. Leave the area as you found it or better.

PART II

THE SACRED EARTH

CHAPTER FOUR

AMERICA: Land of the Sacred Grandmothers and Grandfathers

Of Tirawa himself we know
only that he made all things,
that he is everywhere and in
everything, and that he is almighty.

A PAWNEE SAYING

The American Pawnee Indians are our
spiritual Grandfathers.

BABA RAM DASS

Native American Ecology

At one time, not so long ago, the land that is now the United States of America was dotted with earth lodges, whose doors always opened to the east to receive the first fresh light and life-giving warmth of Grandfather Sun. Buffalo, deer, and elk roamed free. Eagles rode the air currents above the landscape, and the night skies quivered in sparkling splendor. Man lived in conscious recognition of the universe about him, ever walking in the presence of the Great Spirit.

To the Native American, all things told of the Great Spirit, who was called by many names: Tirawa, Wakan

Tanka, Tiowa, and Gitche Manitou. When man sought council with the Great Spirit, he went into the wilderness solitude. He asked for a vision and then waited until an omen, usually an animal, brought the wisdom sought. The Great Spirit sent his messages through the animals. Man, Earth, and all Kingdoms of Life lived in harmony. All was alive.

America faces the twenty-first century with both negative uncertainty and the positive power that comes from its position as a world leader, a power that can be used to create or destroy. Such power must be brought to bear upon the multitude of problems we face. Crime, hunger, overpopulation, the threat of nuclear war, economics. It is hard to say which catastrophe is the most foreboding until one becomes informed as to the condition of the once clean and healthy environment. Our pollution, of Earth, air, and water, has never been at a more critical point, causing ecology to be of paramount concern.

The United States is a country whose pulse beats with the rhythms of the past and the present, ever seeking a balance between the two. It is a powerful country, which resides on some of the most bountiful land on Earth. Modern Americans are a "mixture" of natives and immigrants from all over the world who struggle to live in harmony with the land and the global community of which it is an integral part.

The area of the United States, including Alaska and Hawaii, is a collage of terrains and climate zones ranging from the deserts and mountains of the West, the Great Plains, to the Appalachian Highlands and the Piedmont of the East. The differing climates make for a considerable amount of arctic land, a great spread of temperate conditions, and the small, but significant, tropical areas. Dry climates stand out in strong contrast to the prevailing humid ones.

The country is endowed with both climates and terrains that reflect all three of the Earth's "Life Energies": electricity, magnetism, and electromagnetism. A map illustration is provided at the beginning of each of the chapters on the five countries discussed in this book to give the reader a general view of the manifestation of the

Life Energies in each location. I encourage the reader to use these maps as a general guideline, keeping in mind that "pockets" of differing Life Energies do exist in most areas. On-the-spot application of the Life Energy System must then be applied and you will learn how to do this.

Aside from its natural resources and beauty, the United States has hundreds of planetary vortices, Sacred Sites, and grids that are linked together by a network of corresponding ley lines too numerous to name. Those of us living in the United States have a greater need, perhaps, than any other global citizens to learn how to reconnect to Mother Earth. Our hectic life-styles and consumer-oriented society lead us away from our connection with Nature, but by learning about the power spots and Sacred Sites, most of which were known by the native peoples, we can take the first step toward realigning ourselves with the land.

Native Americans were, and many still are, sensitive to the Earth's life force. The soil was not just "dirt," but the body of the Mother. Commonplace inanimate objects were chosen as sacred tools of planetary connection. The whole story of Nature was honored in a rock, a tree, or a grain of sand. So let us go on a journey of discovery. Let us travel far and wide over the Earth's varied surface in the part of the North American continent that is America.

I have chosen to divide the United States into eight major regions for the purpose of presenting the locations of the primary power spots and Sacred Sites. The regions so divided are: the Southeast, Southwest, Northeast, Northwest, West, Midwest, Hawaii, and Alaska. The regional map on page 72 will give the reader a clear indication of which states are a part of each specific area.

The Earth speaks. Her voice is heard stronger and louder in the vortices and Sacred Sites. We only need to learn to *listen*. Listening takes place with the heart of man, and so it is through the heart that we will hear what the Earth has to say. In the book *The Earth Speaks*, the coauthor, Steve Van Matre, says: "The Earth speaks in the shape of a new leaf, the feel of a water-worn stone, the color of the evening sky, the smell of summer

rain, the sound of the night wind. The Earth's whispers are everywhere, but only those who have slept with it can respond readily to its call.''

Alaska

Alaska has been referred to as ''the land of many faces,'' and rightfully so. It is called Alyeska by the indigenous peoples. The geology of the vast subcontinent is sketchy, primarily due to its great size, which covers thousands of square miles, making it five times the size of Texas. Geologists have been at work to make accurate maps of the state since the end of the nineteenth century. But to produce maps with the same accuracy as we have for the lower forty-eight states would require more than a century! We do know that there are extensive areas of ancient rocks and shallow seas. Alaska's major features were shaped some 135 million years ago by the fusion of crustal plates, advancing and retreating glaciers, climate, and the elevation of sea levels.

The entire region of Alaska is electromagnetic in its Life Energy charge, although there are some ''pockets'' of electricity and magnetism. Albion has identified Alaska as the Spleen Chakra of the Earth. You will remember that the chakras are the main energy points of the Earth's etheric body. This chakra functions as the ''detoxifier'' of the Earth's body, and therefore its role is important to the health of the planet. Also, because electromagnetic energy is balancing or healing energy, he emphasized the necessity of this land being kept in a natural and healthy state. From this we can assume that Alaska can be likened to the *immune system* or source of immunity for the Earth.

The following is a list of some of the major vortices in Alaska:

Mount McKinley: Also known as Denali, which means the ''high one'' or the ''great one,'' Mount McKinley is the highest peak in North America and the second highest on Earth, soaring 20,320 feet into the sky. The moun-

ALASKA

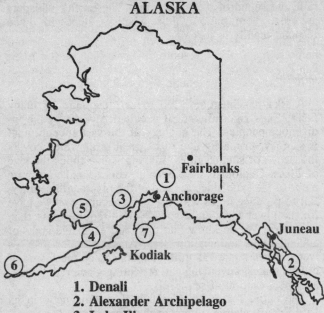

1. Denali
2. Alexander Archipelago
3. Lake Iliamna
4. Becharof Lake
5. Teshepuk and Nakuek Lakes
6. Aleutian Islands
7. Mount Saint Augustine

tain is shrouded in cloud cover much of the year, to the dismay of those who come from all over the world to witness its grandeur. Denali is an electrical vortex and Sacred Site.

Alexander Archipelago: Magnetic grid consisting of hundreds of islands off the coastal mountains of the narrow panhandle in the southeast of Alaska. Remember, a grid is a highly charged location that is not coagulated into an actual vortex. It covers a larger area, and its energy is spread out.

Lake Iliamna: Magnetic vortex located at the head of the Alaskan peninsula, one thousand square miles in area. The largest lake in Alaska. All of the four lakes listed here are located to the south of Anchorage on the Alaskan Peninsula.

Becharof Lake: Magnetic vortex; 458 square miles.

Teshepuk Lake: Magnetic vortex; 315 square miles.

Nakuek Lake: Magnetic vortex; 242 square miles.

Aleutian Islands: Electromagnetic grid located off the southwest tip of the Alaskan Peninsula. Volcanic islands.

Mount Saint Augustine: Electrical vortex. An active volcano located near Augustine Island.

Mention of the Aleutian Islands brings to mind the Ring of Fire of the Pacific. My first awareness of this "rim" of the Pacific Ocean came as a result of Albion's initial comments in the early eighties regarding the Pacific Ocean being an "electric ocean" due to the presence of the Ring of Fire.

"When the Earth was quite young it was first covered by a huge, shallow sea that covered the entire sphere. As the planet evolved, it changed, causing great pressures to be built up. As these pressures were relieved, due to the heating of the core, continents began to appear, built up from volcanic eruptions down under. This continued for millions of years." Albion went on to say that in the basin that is now the Pacific Ocean, there was once a large land mass whose "lid" was blown off, leaving a ring of border land that we now know as the Ring of Fire. The Ring of Fire is a volcanic chain of land, some of it islands, upon which over seventy percent of the Earth's active volcanoes reside. As might be expected, this area is extremely active with frequent earthquake activity. In fact, as clearly stated by geophysicist Louise B. Young in her book *The Blue Planet*: "The entire Pacific Ocean (except for the very southernmost portion) is surrounded by these regions of active Earth movement, which have been dubbed 'The Ring of Fire.' " Young points out that because of this activity, the Pacific is getting steadily smaller; the ocean's floor is being sucked into trenches due to tectonic plate movement. Some of the mass that is sinking is coughed back up in future volcanic eruptions. This, in turn, is believed to be the force and action behind the building of mountain ranges. "The borders of the Pacific are believed to coincide with the boundaries of converging plates, thus creating the Ring of Fire."

The kundalini, the basic human chakra, is located at the base of the spine. C.W. Leadbeater, a leading authority on the human chakras, describes the kundalini as "a devi or goddess luminous as lightning, who lies asleep in the root chakra, coiled like a serpent. . . ." This serpent fire, when aroused through will, rises up the channel in the spine known as the shushumna. This results in greater psychic awareness and clearer insight into the nature of reality. Leadbeater states that the "force of the kundalini in our bodies comes from the laboratory of the Holy Ghost deep down in the earth. It belongs to that terrific glowing fire of the underworld." As the kundalini takes in this "fire," it invigorates and stimulates the evolution of our individual consciousness. When one applies the proper tools of meditation, prayer, ceremony, and personal will to the "awakening" of the kundalini chakra, the slow but steady process of human spiritual growth takes place.

The Ring of Fire, according to Albion, is the single most powerful, most potentially destructive vortex on the contribentire planet. This statement, no doubt, can be attributed to the fact that the Ring of Fire, an electrical vortex, is the site of such phenomenal seismic and volcanic activity. It is also one of the Earth's seven chakra locations, the kundalini. This planetary kundalini, like that same center in the human etheric body, intensifies energy that the Earth "takes into itself" from its spatial environment in the Solar System and galaxy. The circular motion of the Pacific's energy creates a "rise" in the physical activity and the Earth's consciousness. The Aleutians of Alaska and the Cascade Mountain Range are a part of the Ring of Fire vortex/chakra.

Hawaii

Hawaii is truly sacred land. The islands of Hawaii have as a part of their land the southernmost point of land in the United States. The same island is, geologically, the fastest-growing part of the United States. For the last five years the combined forces of spirit and Nature have been building new land from the hot lava pouring forth from the volcano Kilauea, home of the restless goddess Pele.

There are eight major Hawaiian Islands, with a ninth one currently in the making, located in the mid-Pacific off the western coast of North America. The largest of the islands, called the "Big Island," is Hawaii. Hawaii is the home of two powerful volcanoes, Mauna Loa and Kilauea. Geologically, the island is a mere youngster, probably no more than half a million years old. The island is an electrical grid that has several vortices, which will be pointed out later.

Maui, the "Valley Island," is actually two islands that have been fused together by a low-lying isthmus that gives the island its name. The two land areas of Maui are quite different in character. West Maui, perhaps the better-known, is a bustling, extroverted tourist center, while East Maui is sometimes called the "serene child of nature." The easternmost community, Hana, is an intense magnetic vortex and the site of the largest man-built temple in the islands. Some believe Hana to be only a step or two from heaven itself, and that the raindrops are steps that make paradise almost no distance at all. In the *Earth Changes Survival Handbook*, Albion spoke of the Hana area. "Twenty-two miles east of Hana are two of the deepest spots in the ocean anywhere near Hawaii. They are called 'Ka-maka-naho,' which means the deep or hollow eyes." According to nearby residents, it is a sacred place, and no tourist industry has been allowed to operate there. Site of the Seven Sacred Pools, Hana is a beautiful spot.

Maui is an electromagnetic grid, with about half the land being electric due to the terrain around Haleakala

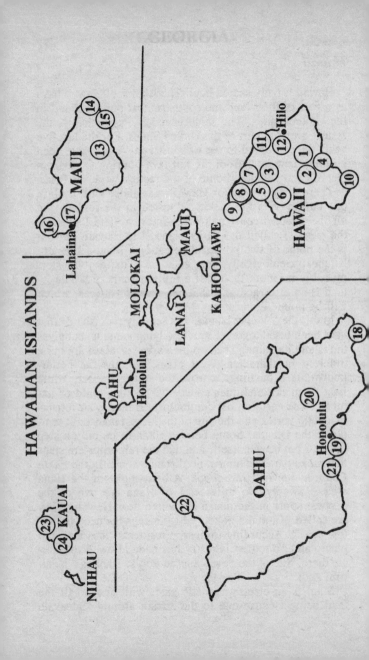

HAWAIIAN ISLANDS

Key: *HAWAIIAN ISLANDS MAP*

HAWAII
1. Mount Kilauea
2. Mauna Loa
3. Mauna Kea
4. Pele's Place, Volcanos National Park, Wahuala Heiau
5. Puu Kohola
6. Hualalai
7. Waipio Valley
8. Kohala
9. Mookini Heiau
10. Southpoint
11. Akaka Falls State Park
12. Kaumana Caves

14. Hana
15. Seven Sacred Pools
16. Honokahua Waterfall
17. Hauloa Stone

OAHU
18. Aiea, Koko Crater
19. Honolulu, Kaena
20. Nuuanu Pali
21. Pearl Harbor
22. Puu O Mahuka, Waimea Falls Park

KAUAI
23. Keei Heiau
24. Waimea Canyon

MAUI
13. Haleakala Crater

Crater, called by the ancients the "house of the Sun." The other half is quite tropical.

The island of Oahu is the site of Honolulu, the islands' capital city, and the famed beach Waikiki. The crush of tourists is so massive there that it can be overwhelming, even to the local business people. Oahu is one of the oldest of the islands, having thrust its head above the sea some 3.4 million years ago. It was, like Maui, formerly composed of two land masses that fused together into a single terrain. The island still bears witness to its dual beginnings, with two parallel mountain ranges—Koolau on the east and Waianae in the west.

Perhaps the island's most famous feature, and a strong electrical vortex, is Diamond Head, a giant crater forged by volcanic activity in a supershort time period, said by some geologists to have been but a few days. Diamond Head is known to the locals as Leahi, "place of fire," clear evidence of its electrical charge.

Three other Hawaiian islands are Molokai, Lanai, and Kahoolawe. Sometimes referred to as the "Forgotten Islands," these three do not receive the same heavy visitor traffic as Hawaii, Oahu, and Maui. Molokai is called the "Friendly Island." Few people outside this island know of the charms of Molokai and its people. In the past, it was called the place of the "living dead," being the remote residence of those stricken with leprosy, a dreaded disease brought by invading westerners. But in the ancient lore Molokai was much more, being the home of the only daughter of Wakea, father of the islands, the goddess Hena. The land bursts majestically from the ocean in a colossal rampart of 2,000-foot cliffs with great valleys overgrown with jungle foliage. Numerous waterfalls, notably the 1,750-foot Kahiwa Falls, constitute natural electromagnetic vortices.

Lanai is pineapple land. Pineapple, second only to sugar, is Hawaii's leading crop. The huge fields are a spectacular sight even from a distance.

Hahoolawe is a small island shaped in the form of a fetus. In the old days it was a retreat site for the kahunas, the knowers and practitioners of the arcane Hawaiian wisdom. The island is now used as a military target range. I understand that there is mounting concern among the kahunas for the safety of the many Sacred Sites on the island due to the violent handiwork of man.

Kauai, called the "Garden Island," is a vast sunlit garden known in the Hawaiian language as "fruitful season." One look tells one why. Kauai is the elder lady of the island chain. Geologists estimate her age to be as much as 5.6 million years, which is nearly ten times as great as that of the Big Island. One of the highest peaks in the state stands on Kauai, the 5,243-foot dormant volcano Kawaikini, another of the many natural electrical vortices in the islands. Perhaps the most distinguishing feature of Kauai is Waimea Canyon. Sometimes referred to as the Grand Canyon of Hawaii, Waimea catches the massive runoff from the rains from neighboring Waiaeale, which is, due to the trade winds, called the "rainiest place on Earth." The canyon walls stand out sharply in colored layers of ochre, rust, and multiple shades of brown, tinted from eons of the residue of volcanic eruptions. The word Waimea means "reddish water." The gorge is 14.5 miles long and 2,857 feet deep. To reach the best view, the visitor must climb up from the cane fields on the lee side, into the cool, misty forests.

Niihau is only seventy-three square miles in size and is the only privately owned island in Hawaii. Owned by the Robinsons, the well-known descendants of an old missionary family, this tiny island is inhabited by approximately 260 native people. Only the native tongue is spoken, and the main source of income for the small population is from the Niihau shells, which are collected and sold. Visitors are not allowed on the island without special permission from the Robinson family. Recent drought and other problems have brought severe economic problems to Niihau, and there is a struggle taking place now for its recovery.

Every traveler to Hawaii must come to know of the kahunas, in order to fully appreciate the Sacred Sites, their meanings and energy. Traditional Hawaiian priests, the kahunas were, and still are, both male and female. These special individuals are selected and trained by predecessors in the spiritual and magical arts that range from healing to weather control. Communication with gods and goddesses and the spirits of the dead and of the elements are all integral parts of the kahuna's powers. These shamans usually remain in the background, but a few are coming forward now to share and teach others of their beliefs and traditions. The kahunas, which means "Keepers of the Secret," were outlawed by the early missionaries, and their knowledge and ways were reduced to mere superstition. However, the magicians have secretly continued their work, and in some isolated districts they have practiced their arts openly.

One kahuna is currently beginning to share, in lecture and workshop format, the basic knowledge of her ancestors. Known to her friends as Pua, this traditional Hawaiian woman speaks fluently and willingly of ancient ceremonies and their meanings, healing knowledge and techniques, as well as many of the various traditions of her ancestors. It is to Pua that I owe the information on the Sacred Sites and vortices in Hawaii, and for this I am extremely grateful. Visitors wishing to contact Pua, whose full name is Wahinealiikukahiliopua, which means "the child that stands close to the Supreme Being," may write P.O. Box 4878, Hilo, Hawaii 96720.

Because of the high volcanic activity in the past and present, much of the Hawaiian Islands is intensely electric, with only the most tropical areas of the islands having any really significant number of magnetic or electromagnetic vortices. There are too many Sacred Sites on the islands to mention here, except for the ones that Pua has shared with us, and these are most special to the traditional people.

Keep in mind that the most notable deity of the Hawaiian people is the goddess Pele, for her presence is the very "soul" of the islands. As I mentioned earlier, the worship of this Polynesian female spirit is ancient. Her spirit is said to inhabit the now-erupting volcano Mount Kilauea, on the island of Hawaii. However, previous accounts place Pele in association with the islands of Kauai, Oahu, Molokai, and Maui as well, during the time that these islands were being built. Pele is the power and force of the volcano. When making a pilgrimage to the Islands, one is certain to encounter the spirit of Pele. To honor this powerful goddess, offerings of food or tobacco are recommended. Pua suggests that liquor, usually gin, is a more suitable offering, for the spirits are particularly fond of alcohol.

The Island of Hawaii

Mount Kilauea: Known as Halemaumau, the Home of Pele, Kilauea has been erupting for the last five years and is the only erupting volcano at the time of this writing. The main crater, Mokuaweoweo, located high atop Kilauea, is said to be the original home of the fire goddess. Kilauea is an electrical vortex.

Mauna Loa: The name translates to mean "long mountain." It is an electrical vortex. The summit has long been a place for sacred ceremonies. If one chooses to make the hike, it is open to the public and is a select site to meditate or do private rituals.

Mauna Kea: Known long ago as the "white mountain," Mauna Kea is the home of the snow goddess, Poliahu. Legend tells of the time when Pele first came to the islands but was chased off by Poliahu. Pele settled at Mauna Loa in the crater of Mokuaweoweo, and later moved to Halemaumau, her current place of worship. Within this crater is Uwe Kahuna, the sacred place where the kahunas go to cry or chant, their way of making prayers. It is still used for this purpose. There is a section specifically used for prayers and offerings, and it is open to the public. This is also an electrical vortex.

Pele's Place (*Puna* and *Kau*): There are many sacred places located within the island sections of Kau and Puna. This is considered Pele's part of the island. One of the most renowned is called Punaluu, where there are sacred cold water pools where people went to purify and cleanse themselves before entering into the ocean for healing. Hawaiians believe that the salt water of the ocean has special healing powers. The pools are a small magnetic vortex.

Puu Kohola: This is the site of the sacred temple of King Kamehameha the First. Only Hawaiians are allowed. However, there is a shark temple here, which is open to the public. The shark has long been sacred to the Hawaiian people, being an ancestral guardian of some of the clans of people.

Haulalai: At present a dormant volcano, Haulalai is one of the five mountains, all natural electrical vortices, on the Big Island. It last erupted in 1801, but is believed by Pua to be ready to erupt again in the near future.

Waipio Valley: One of the few areas that is a magnetic vortex, Waipio Valley is where Kamehameha the First was taken to be reared. It used to be a community of three thousand people and has long been used as a site for ceremony.

Kohala: Kohala is the oldest part of the Big Island. The Hawaiians who come from here or Kau are highly respected, for this area has kept the old traditions. A valley within the Kohala district, known as Pulolu, is the birthplace of Kamehameha and is also the place where he was trained to become a warrior. This is an electromagnetic area and is a good place to go for tapping the "warrior" within. Another town in the Kohala district is Havi. Kamehameha spent a great deal of time here. It is also a site of ceremony. The entire district of Kohala is an electromagnetic grid.

Mookini Heiau: This is the place of the birth stone of Kamehameha, which is now a Sacred Site. The stone is electrical and a good place to go to trigger renewal and rebirth.

Kona: Kona is the location of the City of Refuge built to harbor criminals, who only needed to make it there for safe refuge. It was once the home of Kaahunamu, Queen of Kamehameha, who was the regent or ruler of all the islands. Although not a vortex, Kona is an electrical area.

Southpoint: This is the southernmost point in the United States. It is the location of many sacred and historical sites. The Maoris landed here from New Zealand. A Maori ceremony is still done here in the winter season (January and February) and is open to the public.

Waterfalls: These are all electromagnetic vortices: Kalvahine Waterfall, Akaka Waterfall, Kahuna Falls, and Hiilawe Falls.

The Island of Maui

Haleakala Crater: Haleakala is the third highest mountain in Hawaii. The name means "House of the Sun," and it is the site of an ancient volcano. Some believe the volcano will come to life again in the future. It is an electric vortex.

Hana: This highly magnetic area is a powerful grid that contains many Sacred Sites and natural vortices. It is also the location of the largest temple in Hawaii, erected to the goddess Piilani, deity of the entire island of Maui.

Seven Sacred Pools: These pools constitute, collectively, the most powerful magnetic vortex in Hawaii. The pools contain healing waters and are easily accessible. Pua says that the spirits here are very active. Kiha Wahini is the goddess of the Seven Sacred Pools at Hana. She appears in the mist of the rainbow created by the waters.

Honokohau Waterfall: This is an electromagnetic vortex.

Many of the sacred places on Maui are kept secret but are still being used. They are not open to tourists or to those not brought up in the Hawaiian tradition. In order to preserve their sanctity, such places are private and they should be respected.

The Island of Kahoolawe

This is the infant of the islands and close to Maui. There are several sacred places on the island, but they are kept secret. Special permission must be granted by the U.S. government in order to visit the area. The various kahunas, according to Pua, go to Kahoolawe as a place for refuge.

The Island of Molokai

Puleo'o: This sacred mountain's name translates to mean "power of prayer." It is one of the most powerful of Sacred Sites and is an electrical vortex where the people gathered to pray and chant for protection. Puleo'o is privately owned by Molokai Ranch, but one can visit with permission. It is on the west side of the island. It is believed that all who lived there had great powers of the mind.

Temple of Laka: Laka was a human woman who was taught the hula dance by the goddess Kapo. Many mysterious events have occurred here. Because of Kapo's jealousy of Laka teaching others the hula, sorcery began, so it is said. Albion suggests that this area is a "time warp" type of vortex, and one should take psychic precautions before visiting.

Ili Opae: Located on the east side of the island, this is the site of the second largest temple in all the islands. It is a highly magnetic area, but not a full vortex. Ili

Opae is a place of prayer built after the arrival of a Tahitian chief Paao.

Lanikaula: Lanikaula was a great Hawaiian prophet, and this site is named for him. It is also the location of the sacred Kukui nut grove, a nut which can be used for physical lighting just like a candle, for medicine and food, and for its useful oil. The esoteric value of the nut is as a symbol of enlightenment. This is said by Pua to be a healing area and also a good place for meditation.

Kahiwa Falls: At 1,750 feet, this is the longest waterfall in Hawaii. It is an electromagnetic vortex.

Papalava Falls: An electromagnetic vortex.

The Island of Oahu

Aiea: This is the location of a healing temple. It is here that healing herbs and medicines were prepared by the kahunas who were in charge of this temple. It is a strong magnetic vortex area.

Kaaawa: Located on the windward side of the island, Kaaawa is the site of a valley that houses a most sacred mountain. The Night Marchers are a configuration of rocks that guard this place. Legends say that the spirits walk in this area at night. Kaaawa is generally electromagnetic, but the mountain itself is an electrical vortex.

Honolulu: While it is traditionally known as "the gathering place," not all of Honolulu is a bustling city. There is a place called Kaena in the area. In Hawaiian legends, the spirits of the dead would travel from one island to the other and gather in Kaena before taking the leap to Kauai for purification and reincarnation. The general area is electric, especially now due to the city.

Nuuanu Pali: This is the place where Kamehameha I pushed a lot of the warriors over the cliff, winning the battle that resulted in uniting all the islands together. It is an electrical, man-made vortex.

Kaliuwaa Falls: This is a sacred waterfall and an electromagnetic vortex.

The Island of Kauai

Mount Waileale: This is considered to be one of the most sacred places on Kauai. It is the site of the Temple of Pele and is a magnetic vortex. The site is only accessible by helicopter or by hiking.

Keei Heiau: This temple is another sacred place in Hanalei on the Napali coast. This is a place where the hula students had their graduation. In order to graduate, one had to swim the strong current from the beach area to the first level of the heiau (temple) and then climb to the other levels. This area is called Haena, where the spirits would come for purification prior to reincarnation. Visitors can drive there and then walk the trail. It is an electrical area.

Waimea Canyon: An electromagnetic grid, Waimea Canyon is the Grand Canyon of Hawaii.

Kalalua: Known as the Valley of the Lost Tribes, Kalalua is the name given to the entire area. The Lost Tribes were a tribe of people who disappeared from this area in the seventeenth century and were never seen again. This is another "time warp" type of vortex and is highly magnetic.

Waterfalls: The three main waterfalls on Kauai are Waialaealae Falls, Waipoo Falls, and Awini Falls. All three are electromagnetic vortices.

I have omitted certain islands or areas because they are kept secret and also to respect Pua's desire not to reveal information about some sites. As a special note, the four major gods held sacred to the Hawaiian people are:

Iaonlani: The Creator who gave life to four Emanations who represent Iaonlani's activities and are considered the four main gods.

Ku: the Creator (Master Architect) and Destroyer, the Father.

Kane: the ruler god.

Lono: the son of the ruler god, like the Messiah.

Kanaloa: the god of the sea.

* * *

Hina is known as the Mother Goddess.

If you are able to make a pilgrimage to the Islands of Hawaii, you will truly go on a journey into time. The land of the fire that is Hawaii, with its powerful electrical Earth force, can serve to awaken the inner soul of the Seeker. It can motivate. It can nourish and recharge the body, mind, and spirit. But remember: Go in peace, and in peace you shall return home, renewed and refreshed by the essence of Pele and the life-giving blood of Mother Earth.

The Southwest

The great American Southwest is a harsh but awesome environment due, in part, to the presence of the Mojave and Sonoran deserts, which constitute two huge electrical grids. However, the deserts comprise only a part of southern California, Arizona, New Mexico, and extreme western Texas. Lush green forests, mountain valleys, and streams grace the Alpine country of northern Arizona and parts of New Mexico. Because of the rich Indian cultures in the Southwest, the area is filled with recognized Sacred Sites, some well preserved, that have been acclaimed by various native tribes over centuries. Some of the sites are indeed powerful vortices, while others are grids and ley line terminals. I will begin our identification of the power spots of the Southwest by locating the major ones in Arizona.

The major Indian tribes of the Southwest are: The Yuma, Mojave, Havasupai, Walapai, Yavapai, Pima, Papago, Hopi, Zuni, Acoma, Laguna, Jemez, Santa Ana, Santo Domingo, San Juan, Santa Clara, Taos, Navajo, and the Apache, which consist of the Western Apache, Chiricahua, Mescalero, Jicarilla, Lipan, and Kiowa Apache.

Arizona

Grand Canyon: This is the most magnificent of nature's carvings and one of the largest electrical vortices on the planet. Located some seventy miles northeast of Flagstaff, the canyon is sacred to the Hopi, Navajo, and Havasupai people. Lodging and camping sites, hiking, and mule rides into the canyon depths are available from spring through early autumn. Reservations are advised. Grand Canyon Lodges: (602) 638-2631.

Sipapu: The Grand Canyon is the site of *Sipapu*, the place of "emergence" of the ancient Hopi who had gone underground to live during a major cycle of previous Earth changes. Sipapu is one of the few magnetic vortices, its water source being the Colorado River. Sipapu is located where the Little Colorado and the Colorado rivers meet.

The Grand Canyon is a place where huge numbers of angelic presences can be perceived as it is a gathering place for those Light Beings who have electrical vortices as their charge.

Grand Canyon Caverns: These caves constitute a magnetic vortex and are located twenty-five miles northwest of Seligman on old Route 66, which is now Highway 40. Tours are available.

Twin Rocks: These are located on the floor of the Grand Canyon on the Havasupai Reservation. They are a ceremonial site that serves much the same purpose as Prophecy Rock does for the Hopi.

San Francisco Peaks: Located in Flagstaff and sacred to the Hopi and Navajo, the "Peaks" are volcanic masterpieces of beauty, known to be the "home" of the Cloud People or "kachinas," who are the gods and goddesses of the Hopi. Hiking is permitted. Lodging is available in Flagstaff. Ski lifts are open for viewing autumn colors. The peaks are an electrical vortex.

Sedona: Located approximately 120 miles northwest of Phoenix, Sedona is in beautiful red rock country. Site of seven natural Earth vortices: Bell Rock, electric "beacon" vortex; Boynton Canyon, electromagnetic vortex; Red Rock Crossing, magnetic vortex; Apache Leap,

ARIZONA

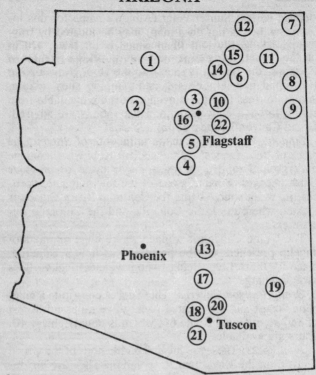

1. Grand Canyon
2. Grand Canyon Caverns
3. San Francisco Peaks
4. Sedona
5. Oak Creek Canyon
6. Hopiland
7. Four Corners
8. Canyon de Chelly
9. Window Rock
10. Sunset Crater
11. Round Rock
12. Monument Valley
13. Superstition Mountains
14. Big Mountain
15. Black Mesa
16. Mars Hill
17. Casa Grande National Monument
18. Picacho Peak
19. Aravaipa Canyon
20. Mount Lemon
21. Kitt Peak
22. Lake Mary and Mormon Lake

electric vortex; Sunset Point (Albion's name for this location, which is not on a map) may be located by traveling up Schnebly Hill Road which is off Hwy. 179 in Sedona. The road is marked clearly by a sign in front of the Horwitch Art Gallery. The road leads to Sunset Point and is mostly gravel, not accessible or safe in the winter, electric vortex; the general area of the uptown post office, electric vortex; Airport Road, electric vortex. Information and maps of the vortex locations may be obtained at the Golden Word Book Centre: (602) 282-2688.

Oak Creek Canyon: Just north of Sedona, it is an electromagnetic grid.

Hunanki: These are ruins of dwellings and kivas of the ancient Anasazi and are located off Highway 89A just west of Sedona.

Tuzigoot: Located in Cottonwood, these are ruins of a ceremonial and village site.

Hopiland: The three Hopi mesas known as First, Second, and Third Mesas are each powerful electrical vortices. For information on dances and lodging, write Hopi Tribal Headquarters, Kykotsmovi, Arizona.

• *First Mesa*:

Village of Walpi: Walpi is sometimes closed to visitors, and a guide must accompany anyone wishing to tour the village. Visitors may inquire at Ponsi Hall on First Mesa.

Snake Rock: a mini electrical vortex.

• *Second Mesa*: This is an electrical vortex located sixty miles north of Winslow. The three villages on Second Mesa where most ceremonies take place are: Shungopovi, Mishongnovi, and Shipaulovi.

Prophecy Rock: Often called Corn Rock by the Hopi, Prophecy Rock is a restricted area and may not be visited at the actual site. The rocks can be seen, however, for miles around. They are located at the end of

Second Mesa. The rocks are a strong electromagnetic vortex known to the Hopi for centuries.

Grey Springs: This is one of the few magnetic vortices on the three mesas. Located on Second Mesa, right on the main road, this is a Sacred Site/spring. The spring is not open to the public.

"Crack in the World": Dubbed this name by a non-Hopi visitor, this is a Sacred Site, once believed to be the area of an ancient river, now underground, and waterfall. Evidence of corn offerings are often seen in this area. Public access. This area is directly across from the Hopi Cultural Center on Second Mesa. Some say this is a sacred area dedicated to the deity, Spider Grandmother.

• *Third Mesa*: Site of Old Oraibi, a village continuously inhabited for over fourteen hundred years. The village is currently open to visitors.

Moenkopi: This is a Hopi village located two miles southeast of Tuba City. It is a ceremonial site and a natural electrical vortex. The name means "the place of running water."

Montezuma's Well: Slightly west of I-17 approximately one hundred miles north of Phoenix, it is a magnetic vortex. There are ancient cliff dwellings nearby that are called Montezuma's Castle. Tours are available.

Four Corners: Considered the Earth's Heart Chakra, the area may be reached by traveling from Phoenix to Flagstaff to Tuba City to Kayenta, then seventy miles to Four Corners. No facilities. Electrical vortex.

Canyon de Chelly: Electromagnetic grid (Chinle) and Navajos' summer home. Site of numerous ancient cliff dwellings.

Spider Rock: Located in Canyon de Chelly, this towering monolith is a Sacred Site named in honor of Spider Woman, the Creator. You can hike there and there are tours available of the entire canyon area. Spider Rock is an electrical vortex and is sacred to the Navajo people, being the site of their emergence from the Underworld. It is also the place where the people first came into contact with Spider Woman, also known as Changing Woman.

Window Rock: This is a Sacred Site to the Navajo people. They know it as a "spirit catcher," which is any rock with a natural hole through it caused by the wind, and is considered an opening into the Spirit World. The rock is a place where spirits deliver prophecy to the people. Window Rock is the capital of the Navajo Nation. Electrical vortex.

Sunset Crater: This is a highly electrical area, the site of ancient lava flows resulting from the last eruption of Sunset Crater some nine hundred years ago. It is also the location of Wupatki Ruins, believed to be the first permanent structures built by the prehistoric Anasazi people. A self-guided tour of the ruins is available. Entrance fee may be paid at the Wupatki Ranger Station. The site is approximately twenty miles east of Flagstaff.

Monument Valley: This is an electric grid twenty-five miles north of Kayenta at the Utah border. Tours and lodging facilities are available.

El Capitan: This is a fledgling electric vortex. It is a part of the general Monument Valley area.

Superstition Mountains: Electric grid. Fifteen miles east of Phoenix. An area of many Indian legends and ancient medicine wheels. You need a guide. Few facilities. Treacherous desert terrain.

Big Mountain: Located in a remote part of the Navajo Reservation on Black Mesa, seventy-five miles from Tuba City, Big Mountain is a high tableland. During the time of the Long Walk in 1864, small bands of Dineh (Navajo) went into hiding in this area and remain there until today. They constitute the most culturally intact and traditional of all the communities of Dineh. Peabody Coal and the Hopi Tribal Council are currently making efforts to relocate the Dineh from this area.

Black Mesa: This is an electrical grid located on the Navajo Reservation.

The Holy Mountains of the Navajos: These mountains marked the Navajo's traditional homeland. They are:

Mount Taylor: Located in the San Mateo Range in New Mexico, this is the holy mountain of the South and is called Tsoll-tsilth by the Navajos. Electrical vortex.

San Francisco Peaks: Located north of Flagstaff, this is the holy mountain of the West. Electrical vortex.

Hesperus Peak: This is the holy mountain of the North and is located in the La Plata Range of Colorado. Electrical vortex.

Blanca Peak: Also located in Colorado, this is the sacred mountain of the East. The exact location of this peak is unknown. Electrical vortex.

Mars Hill: This is a beacon vortex in Flagstaff and is the site of the famous Lowell Observatory, which was founded in 1894. Mars Hill is one of the vortices where one can get in touch with the Star Nation. Electromagnetic vortex.

Grand Falls: This is an electric vortex whose energy becomes electromagnetic during the time of the spring melt. It is located thirty miles northeast of Flagstaff.

Wupatki: These Anasazi ceremonial and village site ruins constitute an electrical grid area and are located twenty miles northeast of Flagstaff.

Casa Grande National Monument: This monument is located on Highway 87 just north of Coolidge. It is Arizona's largest prehistoric ruins of the Hohokam Indians.

Picacho Peak: This is an electrical vortex in Tucson.

Aravaipa Canyon: This ruins area is an electromagnetic vortex. The east trailhead is located off US 70, twenty-five miles northwest of Safford.

Mount Lemon: This is an electrical vortex in the Santa Catalina Mountains on the north edge of Tucson.

Kitt Peak: Located fifty miles southwest of Tucson on Highway 86, Kitt Peak is an electrical beacon vortex with access to the Star Nation. It is the site of Kitt Peak National Observatory.

Lake Mary: This lake is a magnetic vortex located eight miles east of Flagstaff.

Mormon Lake: The largest lake in Arizona, Mormon Lake is a magnetic vortex located twenty miles southeast of Flagstaff.

NEW MEXICO

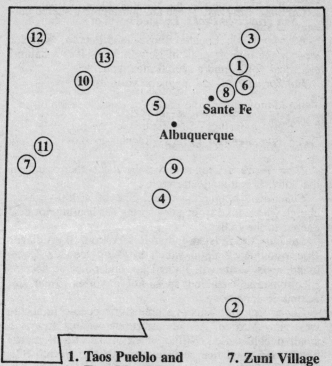

1. Taos Pueblo and Taos Mountain
2. Carlsbad Caverns
3. Wheeler Peak
4. Spence Hot Springs
5. Warm Springs
6. Five Star Hot Springs
7. Zuni Village
8. Chinmayo
9. Los Lunas
10. Chaco Canyon
11. Ma'tsakia
12. Shiprock
13. Blanco Canyon

New Mexico

Taos Pueblo: Powerful electromagnetic grid near the Sangre de Christo Mountains.

Taos Mountain: This is an electrical vortex. It is said to be the emergence point of the ancient native people of the area and is one peak in the middle of the Indian reservation.

Carlsbad Caverns: These are considered a sacred ceremonial site.

Wheeler Peak: Located above Taos Pueblo, Wheeler Peak is the highest peak in New Mexico. It is a natural electrical vortex and a sacred mountain.

Hot Springs: All are magnetic vortices.

- *Spence Hot Springs*—Socorro
- *Warm Springs*—San Ysidro
- *Five Star Hot Springs*—Rancho de Taos

Zuni Village: Albion says that the waters there can heal the body. It is a magnetic vortex.

Chinmayo: Magnetic vortex. Site of a 160-year-old church whose mud from a dry spring has healing powers. Sacred to the Indians.

Los Lunas: San Isleta Indian Reservation. Sky Village. Inscription Rock upon which is found the Ten Commandments written in Phoenician and other alphabets. Electromagnetic sacred spot, not a vortex. Near the Acoma Reservation.

Chaco Canyon: This is a prehistoric pueblo in northwest New Mexico. At the eastern end of this area is a small pueblo called Wijiji, which is the site of petroglyphs and a solstice sun site. An Anasazi Sacred Site called Fajada Butte is also located in Chaco Canyon. Another Sacred Site in this area is Casa Rinconada, which is a kiva. Bonito Pueblo is also located in Chaco Canyon. It is a ceremonial village site of the Anasazi. The area is an electrical vortex. Casual visitors are cautioned about visiting this area, for there is no water there.

Thunder Mountain: Located in Chaco Canyon, this is a sacred mountain to the Zunis, who made pilgrimages there to get in touch with the Sun Father. Electrical vortex.

Huerfano Mountain: This is an electrical vortex and sacred mountain located in Chaco Canyon.

Ma'tsakia: In the Zuni language this name means "sun

shrine.'' It is located three miles northeast of the Zuni Pueblo. Electrical vortex.

Shiprock: This is an electrical vortex which is a shrine and dwelling place of the Old Ones. The Old Ones are the Anasazi Indians who were the prehistoric tribe of this area (the entire Southwest). Anasazi is a Navajo word that means ''the Old Ones'' or ''Ancient Ones.''

Blanco Canyon: This is a sacred ritual site. It is an electrical beacon vortex where one has access to the Star Nation. It is located northeast of Chaco Canyon.

The Northwest

The American Northwest is an area filled with the majesty of Nature. Grandfather mountains, the forests of giant redwoods, rain forests, and scenic wastelands were once home to unique Indian tribes whose cultures and traditions have left their mark on the soul of the landscape as well as modern-day inhabitants.

Washington

Vision Mountain: Vision Mountain is located approximately thirty-five miles east of Spokane and is the present home of the Bear Tribe Medicine Society, headed by Sun Bear, a Chippewa medicine man and internationally known author and teacher. The mountain was sacred to the Kalispels and Spokane Indians. The area is electromagnetic.

Mount Spokane: This mountain is sacred to the Spokane Indians and is located on the outskirts of Spokane. It is an electromagnetic vortex.

Mount Rainier: Mount Rainier, located between Seattle and Spokane, was sacred to the Yakima Indians, who called it ''the mountain that was God.'' Rainier is an electrical vortex. It is a dormant volcano known as ''Grandfather Mountain'' to the native people, and is called Tahoma.

Mount Saint Helens: An active volcano, Mount Saint Helens erupted in May of 1981 after a long sleep. It is an electrical vortex.

Maryhill: Located on the Columbia River, one hun-

WASHINGTON

1. Vision Mountain
2. Mount Spokane
3. Mount Rainier
4. Mount Saint Helens
5. Maryhill

dred miles east of Portland, Maryhill is an exact replica of Stonehenge in Great Britain.

Oregon
   Mount Hood: This is an electrical vortex.
   Gold Hill: This is an area of geomantic phenomena, constituting a "time warp" type of vortex.

The West

   The American West is a land of many terrains, ranging from deserts to mountains, islands to seacoast. It is a land that was once the destiny of pioneers from the East who sought a new horizon upon which to build their lives. The native people of the West were, and still are, a rich source of the West's power and intrigue. Ancient ruins that dot the land hold their secrets in quiet repose and

OREGON

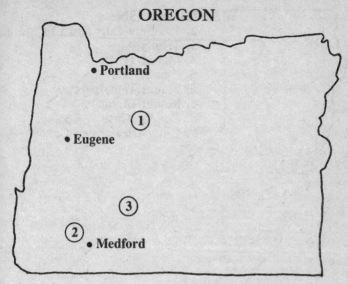

1. Mount Hood
2. Gold Hill
3. Crater Lake

stand as stark reminders of a time and place that comprised the spirit of our beautiful continent.

California

   Cowles Mountain: This is an electrical vortex located in the Cowles-Fortuna Regional Park in San Diego. It is the site of a stone circle.

   Viejas Mountain: This name means "the old women." Sacred to the Kymeyaay Indians, this mountain is an annual ceremonial and pilgrimage site located in San Diego County. Electrical vortex.

   Mount Shasta: Located in the Redding area, Shasta is an electrical vortex. The mountain has a long history of supernatural phenomena associated with it and is sacred to the native people of the area.

   Yosemite Falls: Located in Yosemite National Park off

CALIFORNIA

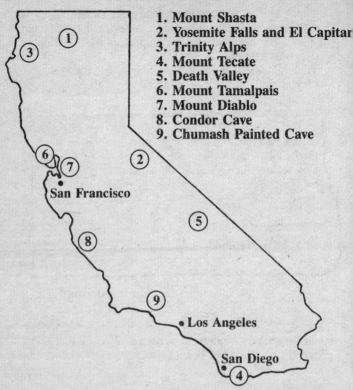

1. Mount Shasta
2. Yosemite Falls and El Capitan
3. Trinity Alps
4. Mount Tecate
5. Death Valley
6. Mount Tamalpais
7. Mount Diablo
8. Condor Cave
9. Chumash Painted Cave

San Francisco

Los Angeles

San Diego

Highway 395 on Route 20, the falls are an electromagnetic vortex. This is a good healing and meditation area.

Trinity Alps: This area is sacred. The native peoples of California used this area for ceremonies and healing, specifically a site known as "Doctor Rock."

El Capitan: Located in Yosemite, El Capitan is a natural electrical vortex.

Mount Tecate: Located on the California/Baja border, twenty-five miles southeast of San Diego, this is a sacred mountain to the Yumas, Cochimas, and other tribes. Its name means "the exalted high place," and it was a place of initiation into the Sacred Sites. Electrical vortex.

Death Valley: A huge electrical grid, Death Valley is one of the hottest places in North America. Legends and rumors alike have set this area apart as the location of underground cities.

Mount Tamalpais: Located in Marin County, this is an electrical vortex that continues to be an Indian Sacred Site and power spot.

Mount Diablo: Located in the East Bay Area of San Francisco, Mount Diablo is a ceremonial site and Native American power spot that is electrical in nature.

Burro Flats: Located in the Simi Hills of the San Fernando Valley, this area contains several shrines with rock paintings that were done by the Chumash people.

Condor Cave: This cave has rock paintings and is sacred to the Chumash. It is located in the Los Padres National Forest.

Painted Rock: This is an ancient Chumash shrine known as the "House of the Sun." It is located on the high grasslands of the Sierra Madre.

Window Cave: This is a Chumash Sacred Site containing petroglyphs. It is located on what is now Vandenburg Air Force Base.

Honda Canyon: This is a natural rock shelter sacred to the native people. It is a place of fertility and emergence. It is located near Window Cave.

Painted Cave: These cave paintings are located near San Marcos Pass in Santa Barbara.

Nevada

Lake Tahoe: This is a large magnetic vortex in an electromagnetic grid area.

Western Shoshone Sacred Sites:

Battle Mountain: This is a part of the Western Shoshones' ancestral land and is currently under dispute between the native people and the Claims Commission.

Pyramid Lake: Housing developments now threaten this Paiute settlement. Magnetic vortex.

NEVADA

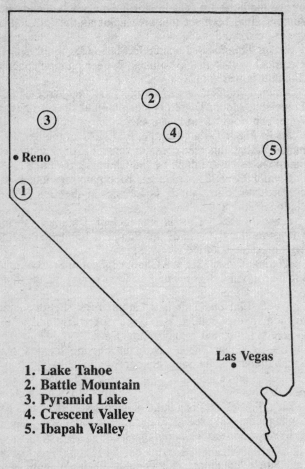

• Reno

1. **Lake Tahoe**
2. **Battle Mountain**
3. **Pyramid Lake**
4. **Crescent Valley**
5. **Ibapah Valley**

Crescent Valley: Also in dispute, this area lies southeast of Battle Mountain.

Ruby Valley: This is a twenty-four-million-acre area
in southeastern California, eastern Nevada, and western Utah. In 1863 the Newe Indians and President Lin-

COLORADO

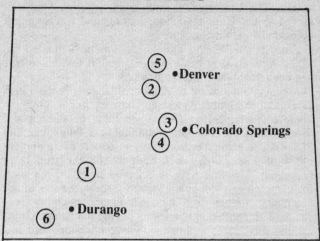

1. Ouray
2. Echo Lake
3. Manitou Springs

4. Pikes Peak
5. Boulder
6. Mesa Verde

coln signed a treaty to insure the safe transport of gold shipments through this area.

Ibapah Valley: This valley is located in the Great Salt Desert at the Utah-Nevada border. The steep ridges of the Deep Creek Range carry good water into this area, which was an ancient territory of the Gosi Ute.

Colorado

Ouray: This town is located in the San Juan Mountain Range northeast of Durango. Electromagnetic area. It is the location of many natural hot springs sacred to the Ute Tribe. Magnetic area.

Echo Lake: Located near Evergreen off Interstate Highway 70, this is a natural magnetic vortex.

Manitou Springs: This electromagnetic area is located just west of Colorado Springs. The springs have healing properties.

Pikes Peak: This is a sacred mountain and an electrical vortex. The Ute creation myth centered around it. It is sacred to the Ute, Arapahoe, Kiowa, and Cheyenne. It is located in Colorado Springs.

Cave of the Winds: This is a magnetic vortex in the Pikes Peak area. It has a peculiar sound resonance that has been witnessed for centuries.

Boulder: According to Albion, this town is the Heart Chakra of the North American continent.

Mesa Verde: Located here are ruins of shrines and dwellings of the Old Ones containing a Sun kiva. The Sun Kiva at Mesa Verde, Colorado is part of an ancient cliff-dwelling site that was built by the ancestral Hopi (Anasazi). The Sun Kiva is believed to have been used for ceremonies. The Hopis regard it to be the site of the legendary temple built by their ancestors, who were struck with confusion of tongues during the construction, leaving the temple unfinished. These ancestors then migrated south and established the present Hopi villages in northeastern Arizona.

Utah

Great Salt Lake: This great body of salt water is an electric vortex, one of the few bodies of water in the entire world that is not magnetic. This is due to the heavy salt content of the water and the surrounding terrain.

Hovenweep Castle: Located where southeast Utah meets southwest Colorado, this solar observatory was built by the Anasazi circa A.D. 1200 and is now sacred to the Utes.

Navajo Mountain: Located in southeast Utah, this mountain is mentioned in Navajo mythology as the place of exile of a disgusting, ugly child. The child was sent there by the Monster Slayer and was purported to have become the progenitor of the Paiutes. In the last century Navajo Mountain has become an area of refuge to threatened Navajos.

UTAH

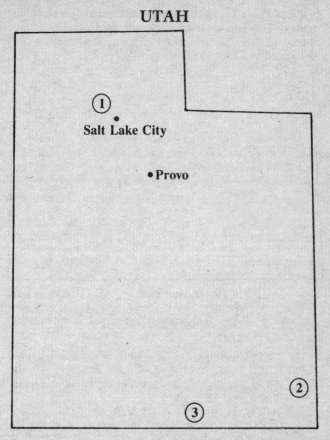

1. Great Salt Lake
2. Hovenweep Castle
3. Navajo Mountain

Wyoming

Big Horn Medicine Wheel: Located near Sheridan, Wyoming, this is a collection of small cairns and spokes. It is 9,642 feet in elevation and is on Medicine Mountain. This medicine wheel was used by the Crow and Cree Indians and is remote and inaccessible most of the

WYOMING

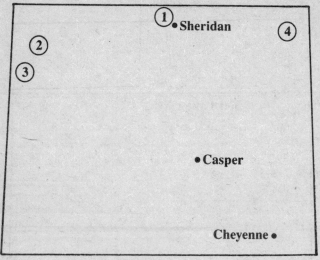

1. **Big Horn Medicine Wheel**
2. **Yellowstone National Park**
3. **Grand Tetons**
4. **Devil's Tower**

year. Approximately fifty medicine wheels are known about at this time. Nearly all of them are found on the east flank of the Rocky Mountains or on the open plains. The rest are located in Canada.

Yellowstone Falls: This is the most powerful electromagnetic vortex in the West. Its waters have healing properties. It is located in Yellowstone National Park.

Old Faithful Geyser: Also located in Yellowstone, this is an electromagnetic vortex. The Yellowstone National Park area contains many natural vortices.

Grand Tetons: These comprise an electrical grid and are located just north of Jackson Hole in the Yellowstone area.

Devil's Tower: This is an electrical beacon vortex and a contact point for the Star Nation.

MONTANA

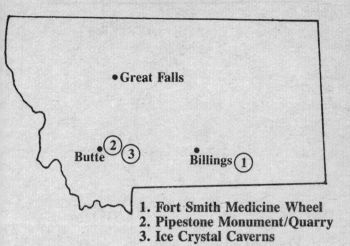

1. Fort Smith Medicine Wheel
2. Pipestone Monument/Quarry
3. Ice Crystal Caverns

Montana

Fort Smith Medicine Wheel: This wheel is located on the Crow Indian Reservation.

Pipestone National Monument/Quarry: This area is sacred to many Native American tribes. It is an electromagnetic vortex and is the site where catlinite is quarried to be fashioned into sacred pipes.

Ice Crystal Caverns: This is a sacred place to the Crow and Cheyenne. It is where they go to perform the Dreamer's Sundance.

The Southeast

Florida

The Southeastern United States is a semitropical land of lowlands, mountains, moist woodlands, and strands of sandy beaches and coves. Once a paradise for the gatherers and hunters who comprised the indigenous people, this is still a land of beauty and peace.

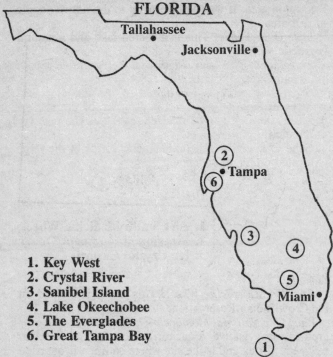

FLORIDA

Tallahassee

Jacksonville

② Tampa

⑥

③

④

⑤

Miami

①

1. Key West
2. Crystal River
3. Sanibel Island
4. Lake Okeechobee
5. The Everglades
6. Great Tampa Bay

Some of the Southeastern Indian tribes are: The Choc-
taw, Cherokee, Catawba, Chickasaw, Creek, Mikasuki,
Seminole, Natchez, Biloxi, Tuscarora, Sugeree, Wa-
teree, Santee, Cape Fear, Waccamaw, Winyaw, Fresh
Water, Pensacola, and the Pascagoula.

Key West: Located on the ocean, this magnetic vortex
is called "the Lip of God." It is sacred to the Seminole
and is the site of much of the human/dolphin communication activity.

Crystal River: This group of six shell mounds is located seventy-five miles north of Tampa on the west
coast. It is an ancient ceremonial and burial site.

Sanibel Island: This island is located in the Gulf of
Mexico off the west coast of Florida in the Sarasota-

Bradenton area. It was a power spot to the native people of that area.

Lake Okeechobee: This is a sacred lake and a natural magnetic vortex.

Everglades: This land is native to the Seminole people and is a magnetic grid.

Great Tampa Bay: This is one of the few electrical vortices in the Southeast and is also one of the few located in water. It is electrical because it is the pathway of a natural lightning belt.

Cape Canaveral: Beacon magnetic vortex at the Cape is located on a huge magnetic grid.

Georgia

Snake River: This river runs through Georgia, Tennessee, and the Carolinas. It was once a sacred river to the Cherokees, but is no longer due to pollution. It was the river where they once birthed their children underwater.

Stone Mountain: Called Lookout Mountain by the native people, this ceremonial site is located near Atlanta. It is an electromagnetic beacon vortex and is a star site that connects one with the Pleiades and the Star Nation people.

Rock Eagle: Near Athens on a mound, this is a very old ceremonial site which is still used by the Creeks. It is a rock shaped like an eagle.

Okeefenokee Swamp: All swamps in Georgia and Florida were considered sacred to the Cherokee and other native people. They were considered "passing over places," the lands where the dead walk. Magnetic grids.

Ywhoo: This is a sacred mound near Helen.

Mississippi

Natchez: The Natchez Indians erected great sun temple mounds here along the Mississippi River.

Yellow Ridge: This is a gathering site near Tupelo.

North Carolina

Lake Junaluska: This is a sacred lake.

Caesar's Head: This is an electromagnetic vortex.

Roan Mountain: This sacred mountain is a sound vor-

GEORGIA

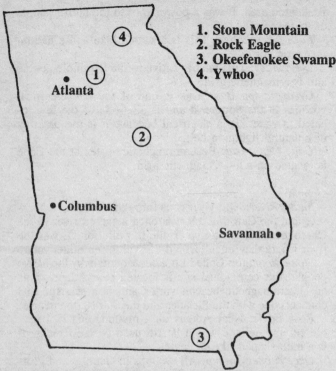

1. Stone Mountain
2. Rock Eagle
3. Okeefenokee Swamp
4. Ywhoo

tex. It is said that after a storm, sounds can be heard coming from the mountain that have been likened to a choir of angels. It is located in Mitchell County.

Blowing Rock: This electromagnetic vortex was once a Cherokee gathering site.

Devil's Tramping Ground: This negative electromagnetic vortex is a perfect circle, forty feet in diameter. Nothing will grow here. It is located at Harper's Crossroads in Siler City.

Franklin: This is a sacred mound site.

Brown Mountain: This is a sacred mountain and the site of unusual light phenomena.

Shining Rock Wilderness Area: This is located in Sylva

MISSISSIPPI

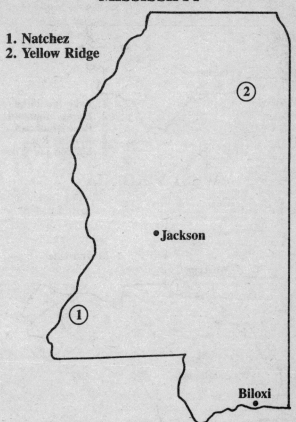

1. Natchez
2. Yellow Ridge

•Jackson

Biloxi

in Cherokee County in the southern Appalachians. The entire southern Appalachian area was held sacred by the native people. It is the oldest land above water on Earth.

West Virginia
   Moundsville: This is the site of a huge, ancient town. The sacred area is all that remains and is now called Grave Creek Mound.

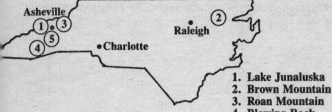

NORTH CAROLINA

Asheville

1. Lake Junaluska
2. Brown Mountain
3. Roan Mountain
4. Blowing Rock
5. Shining Lot Wilderness

WEST VIRGINIA

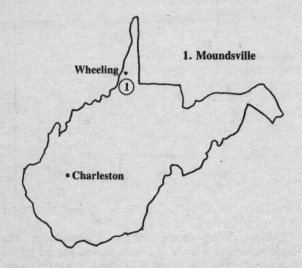

1. Moundsville

Wheeling

Charleston

The Midwest

The Midwest is a land of growth. It is the land of
farmers whose charge it is to be caretakers of the Earth's

soil. The Great Plains spread over vast flatlands, colored gold by waving shafts of wheat, and green by corn, beets, and oats. Midwestern life and culture, forming the moral backbone of America, are a conservative fiber woven into the fabric of contemporary American society. Cold winds sweep across the prairies in winter while the great valleys and hills protect this precious landscape from the elements of Nature.

The Great Lakes: All the Great Lakes were considered great power spots and were sacred to the Chippewa and other native people. I consider each of the Great Lakes a magnetic vortex.

Ohio

Serpent Mound: This sacred solar site is located seventeen miles south of Hillsboro on the north side of State Route 73.

Stark County: Celtic relics have been found in this area, and it is the site of Sun God worship. It is an electromagnetic grid.

Effigy Mound: This is a ceremonial site with huge mounds shaped like animals.

Fort Ancient: Located near Lebanon and Morrow, Ohio, on the Little Miami River. A multimound site. Ceremonial area.

Nebraska

All around the general Omaha area are Sacred Sites along the Loop, Republic, and Platte Rivers.

Four Skidi Pawnee Villages: These villages are sacred sites now on private land.

Pahuk: Located near Cedar Bluff, its name means "Pumpkin Vine Village." It is in the same area as the animal lodge and is the only one of the four villages that can be found at this time and is accessible.

Tuwahukasa: This is the "Village Across a Ridge."

Tuhitspiat: This is the "Village in the Bottom Lands."

Tskvuiara: This is the "Wolf in the Water."

OHIO

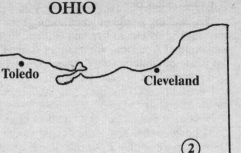

1. Serpent Mound
2. Stark County
3. Fort Ancient

Tower of the Four Winds: This is a recently con structed park built in honor of the Oglala medicine man Black Elk. It is a beautiful and peaceful place located in Blair.

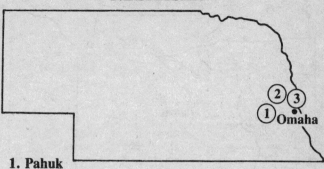

NEBRASKA

1. **Pahuk**
2. **Tower of the Four Winds**

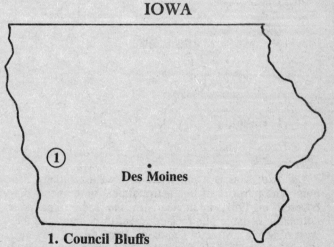

IOWA

1. **Council Bluffs**

Iowa

Council Bluffs: Located on the border area between Iowa and Nebraska, just outside Omaha, Council Bluffs is a site that was the meeting place to discuss peace between the native people and the whites.

ILLINOIS

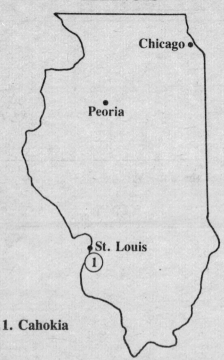

1. Cahokia

Illinois

   Cahokia: This is a sun circle located in southern Illinois. The purpose of this astronomical monument, discovered in 1961, is unclear. In the same area is a collection of large pits located about three thousand feet west of Monk's Mound, Cahokia's largest earth pyramid, which is one hundred feet high. The sun circle marked the equinoxes and the solstices. There are more than one hundred earthen mounds with flat tops in this area. Most are thought to have supported buildings. Some of these mounds are conical. This area is located where the Illinois and Missouri rivers meet.

NORTH & SOUTH DAKOTA

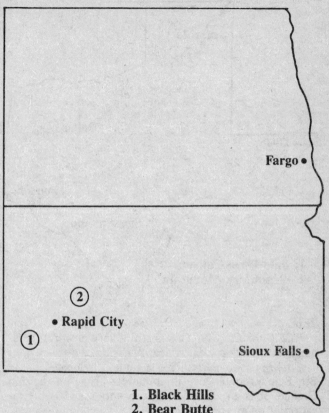

Fargo •

② Bear Butte

• Rapid City

① Black Hills

Sioux Falls •

1. Black Hills
2. Bear Butte

North and South Dakota

Black Hills: This area is sacred to the Sioux and other native people. It is an electric grid.

Bear Butte: Located in South Dakota near Rapid City, Bear Butte is sacred to the Lakota people. It is a place used for vision quests and is an electrical vortex.

TEXAS

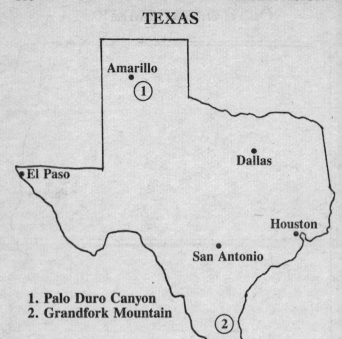

1. Palo Duro Canyon
2. Grandfork Mountain

Texas

Palo Duro Canyon: This is still a very powerful ceremonial site and is located near Amarillo.

Grandfork Mountain: This mountain is located in the
Big Ben National Park in southwest Texas on the Rio
Grande. It is an electrical beacon vortex and is the lo-
cation of many UFO sightings.

Oklahoma

Spiro Mound: This is located near Tuskaloosa. It is the
most powerful Sacred Site to the Western Band of the
Cherokees. It is a gateway vortex that can help one tap
into the dimensions of the ancestors, so it must be used
cautiously. This is the location of a wooden mask of the
antlered god, Cerumnos, and is an electromagnetic grid.

OKLAHOMA

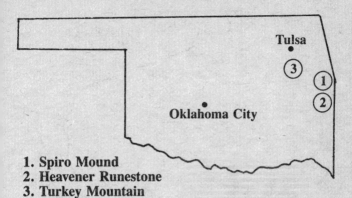

1. Spiro Mound
2. Heavener Runestone
3. Turkey Mountain

Heavener Runestone: This is a Sacred Site located near Fort Smith, Arkansas, on Poteau Mountain. This is a twelve-foot monolith with a runic inscription of eight characters that was possibly used as an ancient sundial.

Turkey Mountain: This mountain is located in Tulsa. It is a sacred rock autographed by Celtic explorers.

Wisconsin

Devil's Lake: This is a magnetic vortex, sacred to the Winnebago people, who honored the warriorlike water spirits that dwell there. The lake is in Devil's Lake State Park in the Baraboo area.

Holy Hill: This is located outside Milwaukee. It is an ancient ceremonial site, now the site of a Christian monastery. It is an electromagnetic vortex.

Minnesota

Blue Mound: This is within twenty miles of Pipestone. It is a sheer cliff that rises out of the plains and a natural electric vortex. Located here is a set of stones in the ground, placed by the native people, that align with the equinoxes. It was here that the native people hunted buffalo by driving them off the cliff.

WISCONSIN

1. Devil's Lake
2. Holy Hill

Tennessee
   Lookout Mountain, Signal Mountain, and Missionary Ridge: These are sacred mountains to the native people of the Chattanooga area.

Kentucky
   Mammoth Cave: Located in Kentucky, this is a natural vortex. On the five levels of the cave are located three rivers, several waterfalls, one lake, and one ancient dead sea.
   Owensboro: Ancient burial site.

MINNESOTA

Duluth•

1. Blue Mound

Minneapolis •

St. Paul •

Pipestone •
①

TENNESSEE

• Nashville

Knoxville •

• Memphis

②
① Chattanooga

1. Lookout Mountain
2. Signal Mountain

The Northeast

The major Native American tribes of the Northeast are:
The Iroquois, Mohawk, Oneida, Onondaga, Cayuga,
Seneca, Tuscarora, Huron, Wyandot, Erie, Susque-
hanna, Passamaquoddy, Abnaki, Penobscot, Pennacook,

KENTUCKY

1. **Mammoth Cave National Park**
2. **Owensboro**

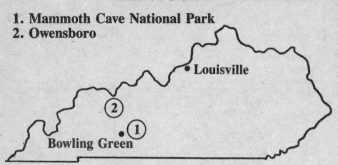

MASSACHUSETTS

1. **Cape Cod**
2. **Lake Wachusett**
3. **Mill River Steel**
4. **The Beehive**

Massachuset, Nauset, Wampanoag, Narraganset, Pe-
quot, Mohegan, Nipmuc, Pocomtuc, Powhatan, Ojibwa
(Chippewa), Menominee, Miami, Illinois, and the Winnebago.

Massachusetts

Cape Cod: A magnetic grid. The whale area.

Lake Wachusett: Located off Route 2 near Princeton,
this is a site used for ceremonies and is a sacred mountain.

NEW YORK

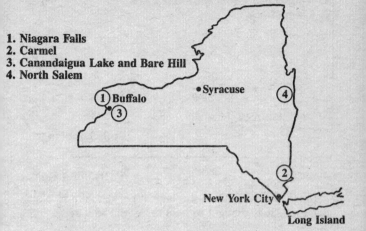

1. Niagara Falls
2. Carmel
3. Canandaigua Lake and Bare Hill
4. North Salem

Mill River Steel: Located near Boston, this is an ancient ceremonial site and burial ground.

The Beehive (Tholos): This magnetic grid area of subterranean chambers is located near Upton.

New York

Niagara Falls: These falls are located in Buffalo on the Canadian border. They were sacred to the Oneida and other native people. They constitute one of the largest electromagnetic vortices in the world.

Carmel: Commonly referred to now as Indian Rock or Turtle Rock, this is a ceremonial site. It is a thirty-foot standing stone with inscriptions of a turtle, an arrow, a bird, and a sun wheel. In the same area is also a huge, flat altar stone.

Canandaigua Lake: Magnetic sound vortex. Sacred to the Oneida people.

Bare Hill: Canandaigua; ceremonial area with many legends connected to it. Iroquois Peacemaker's League meeting place.

PENNSYLVANIA

Allentown •

(1)

•Pittsburgh

Philadelphia•

1. Ringing Rocks

North Salem: This is the largest dolmen site in North America. It is thought to be a memorial to a king.

Pennsylvania
Ringing Rocks: Located near Pleasant Valley west of the Upper Black Eddy on the Delaware River, this five-acre area of rocks is an unusual site with a great deal of electromagnetic power. The rocks are said to ring when struck or thrown.

Vermont
Bellows Falls: Center of town, marked by an inscribed stone. Old gathering place.
Kingdom: Mountains all around. Near the ski area is a place the Indians called the Sugar Bowl, which was a ceremonial site to the Abnakis.
Reading: These are stone temple ruins.
South Pomfret: This is a standing stone site of an ancient fertility cult.
South Royalton: This calendrical site contains standing stones and an equinoctial temple. It is a complex of sacred buildings.
This is an ancient temple site with outdoor altars, phal-

VERMONT

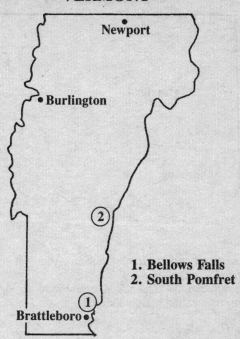

Newport

Burlington

2

1. Bellows Falls
2. South Pomfret

1

Brattleboro

lic monuments, star maps, a fertility altar, and goddess ceiling paintings.

Precincts of the Gods: Located in central Vermont, this is an ancient temple and tomb site. It has a partially buried and collapsed dolmen.

Connecticut

Old Greenwich: Area of many sacred ceremonial sites. A major one is off Catrock Road. This was an Indian village.

Core Rock: Rocky area off the Blue Trail. Two Rocks. Sacred area.

Danbury: There are temple ruins all around this area. It is the site of six megalithic chambers and is an elec-

CONNECTICUT

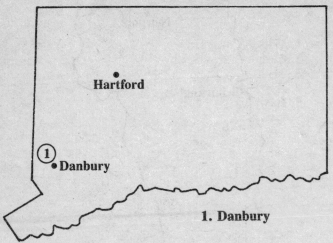

Hartford

1 Danbury

1. Danbury

tromagnetic grid where the Sun God was once wor-
shipped.
  Gunjiwamp: This ancient ceremonial site is a double
stone ring called a Druid's circle.

New Hampshire
  White River (headwater area): At the Vermont and New
Hampshire border, it is the location of many Sacred Sites.
  White Mountain: Sacred mountain.
  Mount Monadnock: Located on Route 137 near Peter-
borough, this is a sacred mountain and ceremonial site
of the people indigenous to the area, especially the Wam-
panoag.
  Mystery Hill: Known as North Salem Mystery Hill and
located outside of the town of North Salem, this is a
megalithic site that is over five thousand years old. It has
been called the American Stonehenge and linked to the
Celts.
  Bartlett: There is a dolmen at this ancient ceremonial
site.
  Raymond: This is a sun temple ceremonial site.

NEW HAMPSHIRE

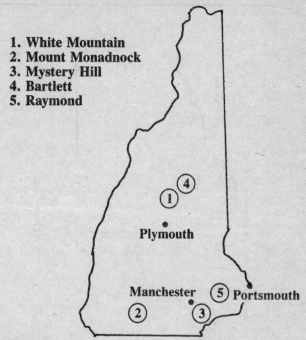

1. White Mountain
2. Mount Monadnock
3. Mystery Hill
4. Bartlett
5. Raymond

Plymouth

Manchester ⑤ Portsmouth
② ③

Maine

Mount Katahdin: This mountain is located in the Baxter State Park and is also a ceremonial area.

Old Town: Many Sacred Sites. Sacred to the Micmac and Penobscot people.

MAINE

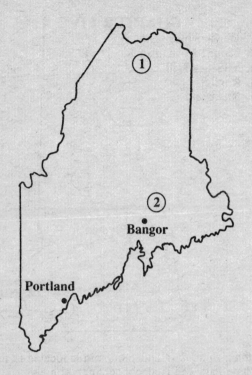

1. Mount Katahdin in Baxter State Park
2. Old Town

CHAPTER FIVE

EGYPT:
Land of Ancient Memories

Angel of Egypt

I am the Angel of Egypt
I guard and protect this ancient land.
My wings stir the memory of a not forgotten past
My consciousness is composed of the tears
And laughter of my human children

I am the Angel of Egypt
I flow through the vein of the land on
  the tides of the River Nile.
I house my Being in the Temples of Man
My heart soars to the chants of the Ancient Initiates

I am the Winged One of the Cradle of Civilization
I am born of the flesh of the ages
I live by the Law of Ra
I dance to the Hymn of Isis

In my pyramids man has passed from death to life
In my pyres burn the pain of growth.
In my soul resides the Essence of the
  kings and queens of the past
In my womb is born the children of the future.

I am the Angel of Egypt
I cause the Sands of Time to rejoice in rebirth

I am nourished by the Nectar of Hope

I am the Angel of Egypt, a Beacon of Pure Light
  that shines in the eyes of my people
I am the Great Holy One who speaks through
  the Silent Voice of the Guardian Sphinx of the desert
By the power of Love I exist.

Albion
October 1987

Egyptian History and Geography

It is impossible to go to Egypt without feeling a strong
connection to the ancient past. The Arcane Mysteries sat-
urate the hot desert air with a lingering silent voice that
seeks ears to listen to their safeguarded wisdom. Egypt
is one of the most desirable pilgrimage sites in the world.
Many people go there for the pleasures of sight-seeing,
while others go with more spiritual intentions. I know of
several people who, upon their arrival in this ancient
land, were able to attune to personal past life experiences
and memories. Still others have reported becoming aware
of a deeply rooted sense of "belonging" to the land and
to the past that resulted in general enlightening, uplift-
ment, and recommitment to their spiritual path. In no
other place do the voices of the ancient gods and goddesses beckon stronger to the human soul.

Who are the Egyptians? Where did they come from?
The answer is simple. No one really knows. What we do
know is that in prehistoric times the area of the Nile
Valley was inhabited and rich in forest and animal life.
Egypt has changed, remolded time and again by time and
climate. Ruins and records of this ancient land tell a story
of a truly unique civilization, one that may have been far
more sophisticated than we have imagined. Some four
thousand years prior to the birth of Christ, the people of
the fertile valleys along the Nile built a great pyramid
whose technology cannot, even today, be duplicated.

EGYPT

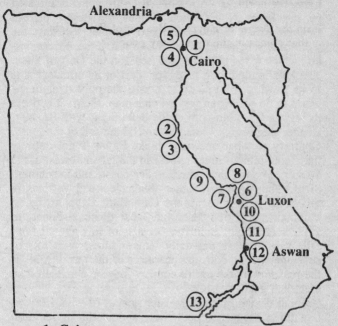

1. Cairo
2. Hermopolis
3. Tel el Amarna
4. Sakkara
5. Giza
6. Luxor
7. Valley of the Kings
   and Queens
8. Denderah
9. Abydos
10. Esna
11. Edfu
12. Aswan
13. Abu Simbal

They originated the first paper, called papyrus, and kept wonderful records of their lives and religious beliefs. They mummified their noble dead by a process that still eludes us. The religion of the Ancient Ones was the most powerful influence upon their lives, with the possible exception of the Nile itself.

Officially known as the Arab Republic of Egypt, modern Egypt is far different from its ancestral past. Occupying the northeast corner of Africa, Egypt is dominated by the River Nile, which divides the desert plateau through which it flows into two unequal sections: the western desert, which borders Libya, and the eastern desert, which extends to the Red Sea and the Gulf of Suez. The Nile is the blood of Egypt. Part of its uniqueness is in its flowing from south to north, the only river in the world to do so. When viewed on a map, the river appears to form a lotus blossom at the delta area, with its long, slender stem firmly rooted in the Nubian soil of the south. Contrary to what one may think, Egypt is not entirely flat. Mountainous areas appear in the far southwest of the Western Desert, along the Red Sea coast, and in southern Sinai. There are two rather weak electrical vortices in this area, known as Mount Catherine, Egypt's highest mountain, of 8,668 feet, and Jabal Shaib al-Banat, of 7,173 feet. Egypt's climate consists of low annual rainfall, varying seasonal daily temperatures, with lots of sunshine. Along with the character of the terrain, this is the reason why the entire country may be considered an electrical grid.

Tomb drawings give us exact images of what life was like three thousand years B.C., and in the agricultural areas to the south of Cairo it goes on the same today. Donkeys trot along solemnly, ears flopping gently to the staccato beat of their feet. Camels look aloof and bear incredible loads, padding softly on cushioned feet. Crops of cotton, sugarcane, alfalfa, and grain still grow in the lush, layered soil that the annual flooding of the Nile maintained for centuries until the High Dam at Aswan changed all that.

Egyptians refer to the Nile-enriched portion of their country as the "Black Land," and the ever-encroaching sandy desert as the "Red Land." Every spring the vicious winds arrive, driving more of the red sand across the fertile black land and making farmers rush to claim back their hold on the green ribbon of soil that borders the Nile. The *shaduf*, the ancient and tedius method of taking the Nile's water to irrigate their crops, is still used today. An ox silently plods a circle that turns the wheel that irrigates the waiting fields.

Cairo, Egypt's capital and Africa's largest city, is a wonderful and intriguing place. Within its boundaries are more Islamic treasures than are found in any city in the world. Like most metropolitan areas, Cairo is a huge man-created electrical vortex. The city never seems to sleep. Filled with ancient temples, old churches, and mosques, this country of forty-six million people revolves around its cities of Cairo, Alexandria, Luxor, and Aswan.

Cairo is a unique mixture of the ancient and modern worlds and literally "swarms" with its fourteen million inhabitants. Truly an international crossroads, Cairo is the meeting center of Africa, Asia, Europe, and Arabia. Everything is controlled from Cairo, which functions as the country's hub for economics, politics, and cultural, military, educational, transportational, and historical affairs.

On my two visits to Egypt, Cairo has been my favorite city. The intense activity, the wonderful bazaars tucked away in every corner, and the gentle smells of spices mixed with the scents of a modern technological society give a flavor that is unforgettable, to say the least. Modern Cairo is the latest city to develop in its location from many Cairos of the past. Actually, the age of the city is not known, and neither are its founders. The oldest part of the city, called Old Cairo, is the site where the Persians built a fort on a strategic point on the Nile. Later, the Romans strengthened the fort and called it Babylon. It could be said that Egypt, including Cairo, has changed more in the last half century than it did in the preceding five thousand years.

Cairo is huge. You cannot really appreciate its size until you try to get around. Driving in the city is not advisable, nor is touring alone. If you go to Egypt alone or with a companion, it is suggested that you join an organized group, at least on your first visit. This is not only cost-effective, but you will stand a better chance of seeing the essentials of the city in a more reasonable amount of time. If you do not care to join a group, I have found that taxis are for hire for private tours of the city for a minimal fee. The cab drivers are quite friendly, and almost everyone who works in the area of tourism speaks English as well as several other languages, including French and Spanish. However, Egypt is a bartering society, and it is a good idea to set the fee for tourist services in advance of your outing. In some of the locations of special interest, such as the pyramid complex at Giza, donkeys, carriages, and camels are also available for hire, but the same rules of agreement of payment should be followed. There are regularly scheduled sight-seeing tours available through your hotel.

Two attractions that must not be missed are the sound and light show at Giza, and the Cairo Museum. A full day at the museum would not be too much time and may not be enough. The Tut collection is incredible. The mummy room, which was closed by Sadat several years ago, is supposed to be reopened soon. The mummies are the actual people whose life stories cover the walls of temples from one end of Egypt to the other! Looking on the faces of Seti I and Ramses II puts everything else in perspective. They lived!

The Egyptian people are definitely a tremendous part of the color and flavor of the country. They are good-natured and friendly, and they like Americans. Relationships between the two countries have greatly improved since 1975, when the Egyptian president, Anwar Sadat, visited the United States, beginning a new phase in the relations between the two countries. Egyptian people are very accommodating to visitors to their country. There is, however, a wide gap between the educated, urban Egyptians one encounters in Cairo and the majority of those living in the more remote areas along the Nile. Many of these people have never been out of their quaint villages or experienced anything other than their way of life, which has changed only slightly over many thousands of years.

Egyptians are demonstrative people! They are constantly touching, hugging, slapping, and kissing one another, for to them, physical contact is a language unto itself. However, this can be misleading. The men hug each other, but there are very strict taboos about men even touching women in public. They are jovial, easy-going, hardworking people who enjoy life as it comes. One of the most important lessons we can learn from them is to be happy with whatever we have. They do it very well. When they happen to be overpaid by some grateful tourist, they immediately seek out friends or family to share their good fortune. If, on the other hand, someone is miserly, they will accept that, too, with only a trace of a frown. Likewise, they are family-oriented, extending a great warmth and love to their children. Perhaps the one thing that westerners will find the most exasperating to deal with is the Egyptians' total disregard for time. Once you get used to it, you will relax and accept it as an integral part of the charm of the people. The key to enjoying both the land and its people is to make an effort to adjust to their way of life rather than demanding that they adjust to yours.

Perhaps the first thing that strikes you upon arrival in Egypt is the poverty. However, when you consider the incredible odds against which Egyptians have struggled, an awareness of their accomplishments will quickly replace any pity or repulsion with empathy and compassion. After centuries of being ruled by other nations, Egypt and its destiny are, at last, in the hands of Egyptians. Their love and pride in their country is evident in their conversations, and they are eager to share their land and their heritage with multitudes of visitors.

No one can truly understand Egypt's people without understanding the religion, which has developed slowly over centuries. The current religion has only come about after many changes, including the country's early conversion to Christianity in the time of the Apostles. The Egyptian Christian Church (the Coptic Church) left very few of the ancient religious practices intact. Even after the Islamic conquest in A.D. 641, many Christian elements have survived in the form of belief in saints and various superstitions. Islam, based on the teachings of the prophet Muhammad, is now the religion of modern Egypt. Generally speaking, it teaches man's submission to God, a belief in angels, sacredly revealed books, particularly the Koran, and the last Day of Judgment. The religion of Islam makes the Egyptian people one of the most crime-free in the world. They truly do practice their faith and are proud of its teachings. The journey to Mecca is the ultimate hope of each person. When one member of a family makes that journey of faith, in many of the rural areas it is proclaimed with signs painted on the family's stucco home. The celebration of Ramadan is a whole month of disciplined fasting, with adults taking no food or water from sunup to sundown. Daily prayers are still a way of life. The courtyards of homes, businesses, and mosques fill with men in prostrate prayer when the call comes from the minarets high above the city. To westerners, Islam can seem strange and spiritually unfamiliar, so it is a good idea for you to be informed about the ways of the Orthodox Moslems prior to going to Egypt. A book that I recommend for gaining an understanding not only of the religion of Islam but of the people as well is *A Woman of Egypt*, by the former first lady, Jehan Sadat.

Sadat's book addresses another issue that can be a source of confusion for westerners, particularly Americans, concerning the role of women in Egyptian society. The Koran allows men to have as many as four wives, but also demands that they be treated equally. The idea of multiple wives can be difficult for westerners, but because of the expense involved and the changes taking place in society, this practice is rapidly disappearing. The struggle for women's rights began in the 1930s and continues today. Women's primary concern seems to lie in the area of education, a right not afforded in times past. Women are also entering the work fields in greater numbers, thus becoming greater economic assets to their families. Today, opportunities are opening for women in the field of government, with a few having held high cabinet positions and seats in the National Assembly in recent times. As women have become more self-sufficient, they have adopted a more westernized mode of dress, and in large metropolitan areas they seldom wear the traditional long, black dresses and head coverings. However, rural customs still embrace the practice of married women dressing only in black, while children and unmarried women are allowed the freedom of brighter colors. Some women still wear a veil across their faces, but most wear only a head covering.

Egypt is a country that can be a year-round travel destination, although the summers are quite hot with temperatures soaring well over one hundred degrees Fahrenheit. Therefore, October through May are the months to travel in more tolerable temperatures. Aswan and Luxor in the south, called "Upper Egypt," are considered the winter resort areas.

The following is an indication of the locations of vortices, grids, and Sacred Sites in Egypt. The Sacred Sites, it might be noted, of modern-day Islam and the Coptic Church, with the one exception of Zeitoun, are not mentioned. These are, for the most part, churches, and are too numerous to mention. However, I have listed specific Sacred Sites that may hold particular interest to the traveler to Egypt.

Beginning with Cairo itself, the entire city is an electrical grid, quite intense in its power and generating a constant flow of pure electrical force. It is filled with Sacred Sites that have been used as places of worship for centuries. Because of the prayer energy generated by people over so long a period of time, most of the sites are man-made vortices rather than Earth vortices. If you visit Cairo, pace yourself well and take time each day for rest and recuperation.

Sacred Sites in Cairo

The mosque is the "church" or temple of Egypt. In Cairo there are more than five hundred mosques, some representing the world's most elaborate examples of Islamic architecture. Some are more famous than others, such as the Muhammad Ali Mosque within the compound of the Citadel, a former fortress constructed with stones from pyramids at Giza. The site of a mosque would certainly qualify as a Sacred Site, but the only one I would consider an actual vortex would be Al-Azhar, "the splendid." Over a thousand years old, Al-Azhar is both a spiritual center and one of learning. Its university is considered the oldest in the world and has educated some of the most influential scholars in the Moslem world.

Mosques are open to visitors, but it is not advisable to go during prayer times. There is a small fee for entrance. Visitors are also asked to cover their feet instead of removing shoes, and cloth slippers are provided for this purpose. Women should also cover bare arms with a scarf or by wearing long-sleeved clothing, which is not provided.

The following is a list of some of the most well-known mosques in Cairo:

Amr ibn el-As: Located in Old Cairo, this mosque dates back to the seventh century. This was the first sacred place to Moslems in Egypt, giving this mosque a particularly strong sacred energy.

Ibn Toulun: Located in the area of the Citadel, Ibn Toulun is considered to be the oldest mosque in Cairo, its building not altered since A.D. 879.

Al-Azhar: Standing on the same site in the district of Al-Azhar for over a thousand years, this place of worship and center of learning is one of the grandest examples of Islamic architecture in the world. It is also an electrical vortex.

Muhammad Ali: Located in the Citadel compound, this mosque was designed by a Greek architect from Turkey and is a reproduction of a mosque in Istanbul.

El Aqsunqur: Known as the Blue Mosque, El Aqsunqur is located in the Bab Zuweila area of Cairo. Its name comes from the blue and green panels of Persian tiles that decorate the east wall.

One definite vortex area in Cairo is the large burial ground called the City of the Dead. Consisting of numerous mosques, tombs, and mausoleums, this area is an electrical vortex and can be difficult to remain in for a long period of time. Its energy is quite intense and can be overbearing, causing a sort of mild electrical "numbness," which is usually interpreted as overtiredness, mild emotional distress, and can produce feelings of hunger and drowsiness and/or energy drain.

Outside the city of Cairo, in Hermopolis, on the west bank, twenty-four miles south of Minya and west of Mallawi, is the site of a temple. This village is a full day's side trip, being about four and one-half hours outside of Cairo. Hotel facilities are minimal, so it is wise to check in advance for reservations. Its distinguishing features are the statues of huge baboons that support the ceiling. Hermopolis is a strong electrical vortex and is the city whose patron was the god Thoth.

Thoth is one of the ancient Egyptian gods most well-known to metaphysical students and those who have studied a bit of the old religion. He embodies a great deal of power and healing and wisdom. He is sometimes referred to as Hermes, thus the name Hermopolis of the village. He is also the chief deity of scribes. In this powerful vortex area it is possible to attune yourself to the records of times past of this arcane land and people.

Another side trip from Cairo can be experienced by a day's journey to the famous Tel el Amarna. This was the city of Akhenaten and Nefertiti. The ruins of the Palace of Nefertiti are a part of the remains, and many tablets in cuneiform writing have been found here and since removed for display in the Cairo Museum.

Tel el Amarna is a very powerful electrical vortex. Perhaps it was chosen as the place for dwelling by its illustrious occupants due to its potent power. After abandoning Thebes, now Karnak, the old capital, Akhenaten and Nefertiti embraced a new worship of one god, Aton, representing a profound change in the religion and consciousness of the people and times. Tel el Amarna can be reached by driving eight miles south of Mallawi and crossing the Nile. Ferries run throughout the day.

Sakkara: About twenty miles southwest of Cairo lies Sakkara, the City of the Dead. This is the location of Zoser's stepped pyramid, believed by some to be older

than the Great Pyramid at Giza. Zoser's is built over a
powerful electric vortex and is reputed to be the site of
ancient fire rituals. The complex contains over fourteen
pyramids and hundreds of tombs dating back to the Thir-
tieth Dynasty. Some believed that the stepped pyramid
represented a stairway to heaven. The energy here tends
to elevate the consciousness to a high degree. I personally found this area to be one where I experienced a need
for ceremony. It gave me a definite sense of the high
rituals that had taken place here, and I felt an ability to
attune to a higher deity much easier than usual. The pyramid was built in 2630 B.C. by Imhotep for Zoser. It was
the first stone construction, and the pillars were built to
imitate bundles of reeds, because reeds were the usual
type of construction at that time. The entire complex is
a duplicate of whatever had been used before, including
wooden doors with hinges, but none move!

The Serapeum: Nearby Zoser's Pyramid is the Serapeum, enormous underground tombs built for the sacred
Apis bulls, which were symbols of life and rebirth. Each
bull "reigned" until the next sacred bull was found, usually a period of fourteen years.

Zeitoun: At one time, before the growth of Cairo, this
was a strong magnetic vortex. The site is now the location of the Coptic Church of Saint Mary, where the miraculous apparitions of the Holy Family appeared in 1968.
The vortex is still intense at times of sacred Christian
holiday celebrations. The church is in Zeitoun, a suburb
north of Cairo, and is easily accessible by taxi. The sanctuary is open to visitors for prayer and meditation.

Pyramids and Sphinx at Giza

Man has left nothing behind him that has challenged
our intellect and our intuition more profoundly than the
Great Pyramid. Located nine miles west of Cairo in the
city of Giza, the pyramid complex is composed of three
gigantic monuments, surely the ultimate pilgrimage experience. The past comes to life when one views the

magnificent solar boat exhibit at the Great Pyramid complex at Giza. Built and *laced* together with ropes, the water craft took fifteen years to reassemble. It was necessary to make duplicate, miniature pieces of the original disassembled boat and work with them, because the original timbers began to dry and warp. A special three-story air-conditioned building was constructed to display the boat. It still smells like cedar, five thousand years later! It is speculated that Cheops was brought to his pyramid tomb in this boat; however, several more solar boats have been discovered and long since removed from their crypts at Giza. A solar boat, similar to the one in the museum, was found still entombed in 1987. A National Geographic team used laser drills with fiber-optic cameras to peer through tiny holes in the age-old resting place of the boat. The team determined that cracks had admitted water and insects, so the boat's encasement was resealed and it is apparently not going to be exhumed. The Giza Plateau itself is a huge electrical grid, but the actual site on which the Great Pyramid is built is a natural electric Earth vortex. One is overwhelmed by the size alone of these great monuments. I do not believe for a moment that they were just tombs, but were places of initiation. Powerful emotions are stirred by the sight of the pyramid(s), emotions that can range from awe to utter intimidation.

In the *Earth Changes Survival Handbook*, I presented a statement given by Albion on the Great Pyramid:

> "There are three areas on Earth that are sound currents, creating *sound* vortices, which wail as they come from the bowels of the planet. These 'sound' energies are primarily produced by deep underground magma flows and the movement of the Earth itself in its orbit, and the geological history of the area. One of these is underground in the continent of Africa in Egypt and the Great Pyramid is built over the top of it. If you were to look at this vortex with the clairvoyant sight, it would appear as two pyramids with their bases together, one below ground, one above."

Albion went on to say that due to the intense vibrations of a "sound" vortex, such places propel the aspirant into an altered state of consciousness very quickly. Assuming this is so, it may account for at least one of the reasons why the Ancients chose that specific place for the most phenomenal engineering feat man has succeeded in accomplishing.

I have spoken to many people who have spent the night in the King's chamber of the Great Pyramid. Some have reported breakthroughs into their own human memory banks, recalling personal experiences but seeing them in a completely new light. Others tell of hearing voices from the past, perhaps chants of initiates or other Wise Ones that still resonate in the psychic reservoir of the chambered stone monument. My own personal feelings involved my sensing, on a deeper level than ever before, my human roots, my ancestry within the human race, my inherited past, which gave me a conscious and secure feeling of "belonging."

The "silent guardian of the desert," the Sphinx, is no less a thought-stirring sacred shrine than the pyramids. Situated but five hundred feet southeast of the Great Pyramid, the Sphinx lies on the desert floor, with the body of a lion, the symbol of kingship, and head of a man, depicting intelligence. One hundred ninety feet long and sixty-six feet high, this wonderful statue faces east, catching the first rays of life-giving sun every morning. The Sphinx's energy is highly electrical, as it sits on the Giza Plateau electric grid. The age of the Sphinx is taking its toll, as chunks of it have fallen away and have had to be replaced. My own feelings while standing between the paws of the sphinx are that the eyes have seen the history of man, down through the ages. In the psychic and physical senses it is the site of ancient "records" that, someday, will reveal a part of the past that will fill in the gaps of our knowledge of our ancestry. I also felt a strong sense that there is a great subterranean network of tunnels beneath the Sphinx and pyramids complex, some, perhaps, extending as far as to Sakkara! There are certain areas to the south, between Giza and Sakkara, where horses will not travel because they become "spooked." The reason for this remains a mystery.

After leaving Cairo, one should also explore other parts of the country, especially Upper Egypt, the location of the two major cities of Luxor and Aswan. Daily air travel is available to the south, as well as the train, a slower but very comfortable overnight trip. The truly daring traveler might consider hiring a car and driver to see the sights along the way, but the distance is several hundred miles, and accommodations can be a problem.

Wherever you go in Egypt, you are accompanied by the ever-present Nile. The river and its many tributaries are truly the magnetic life blood of the land and people, and they form a long magnetic grid system. Sitting by a river recharges one's magnetic energy, calms, and relaxes the tired and tense muscles and nerves of a weary traveler. I also suggest staying near the Nile. It is a good idea, especially for travelers not used to an electrical climate and terrain, which can so quickly deplete energy.

Luxor

Luxor is located on the east bank of the Nile some four hundred miles south of Cairo. Known at one time as Thebes, Luxor was the capital of Egypt during the times of the Middle and New Kingdoms. The ancient ruins of huge monuments, temples, and statues are some of the most magnificent in Egypt. The museum in Luxor contains some of the finest artifacts in Egypt in its very modest building. One of the charming things about this city is its horse-drawn carriages, which provide an inexpensive means to get around to the various sites. The sites that are vortices include the following:

Temple of Luxor: Located in the city of Luxor by the Nile, this temple was built during the reign of Amenhotep III and was dedicated to the Holy Trinity: Amen-Ra, Mut, and Khonsu. An avenue of sphinxes once connected Luxor Temple with Karnak, both the sites of one powerful and large electromagnetic vortex. Good healing energy is found here. Obviously a site of worship, Luxor was also spoken of by Albion as being a temple of initiation and of study. The Luxor Temple is built over a two-mile-long avenue that once led from the Karnak Temple to the sister Temple of Luxor. The ancient festival of Opet traced that distance as the statue of Amen-Ra, deity of Karnak, was brought by barge down the river to the Temple at Luxor every summer during the rising of the Nile's tide. For twenty-four days, the people celebrated the Nile's promised bounty with feasting and dancing.

Karnak Temple

Built on a Sacred Site recognized by the ancients, Karnak is also the site of an electric ley terminal. The sacred lake on the premises is one of the few magnetic vortices in Egypt. The temple complex covers four hundred acres. An avenue of ram-headed sphinxes, which used to be much longer, is reminiscent of "stone avenues" leading up to megalithic sites in Britain that are also associated with a water source. The Temple of Karnak in Luxor is the largest temple complex in the world. Each pharaoh added to the total number of buildings, statues, columns, steles, and sacred artifacts in the temple. The entire Notre Dame Cathedral would easily fit inside the portion of Karnak Temple known as the Hypostyle Hall. In that section, there are 136 columns in sixteen rows, each large enough for one hundred men to stand at the top. It takes one dozen people holding hands to surround one column at the base. The sound and light show at the Karnak Temple gives the visitor the opportunity to see the temple complex as if he were participating in a ceremonial event. Beginning at the avenue of sphinxes that line the entryway, the observers are led from point to point inside the courtyard as a perfectly timed series of lights and voices bring to life the past history of each fascinating spot. Finally the audience assembles in the tiers of seats beside the sacred lake and views the temple complex as the history of Karnak is told in words and music.

Karnak is located about two miles north of Luxor. The entrance from the road along the Nile is known as the North Gate of the Great Temple of Amen-Ra. This deity was the patron god of Thebes. There are many who feel, from archaeological evidence, that this was perhaps the most important temple in Egypt.

I am inclined to agree, because Albion made reference to an intensely potent magnetic vortex, one of the few in Egypt, located on the grounds of Karnak, known as the sacred lake. The lake itself is quite large, and its actual depth has yet to be determined; neither has its use, if any. Albion's comments suggested that the lake's purpose was to supply a source of pure magnetism, which, in turn, "recharged" the etheric body of the initiates, whose work involved spending tremendous amounts of such energy. The lake also served as a ceremonial site.

Albion talked about four specific types of priests who were trained at Karnak. There were only a few of these priests at any given time, but many "teachers" or "instructors" who lived in the complex. One of the types of priests was the *Diviners*, who were taught the fine art of dowsing. Finding water sources and predicting events regarding water such as flooding and drought, and plagues or illnesses connected with water, seemed to be the task. Considering the climate and desert terrain in which the people lived, the task was an important one. The animals (totems) sacred to this order of priests were the crocodile, horus hawk, fish, and the black ibis. Another type was called the *Stargazers*. They concerned themselves with the sky and were highly educated in the current science of astronomy. All that went on in the heavens was of concern to these priests, for such events were considered as portents and omens and interpreted in that way. The information gained served as prophecy and as tools of interpreting major events on Earth. Then there were the *Healers*. These specially trained initiates became experts in several areas of the healing arts, assisted by the use of herbs and ointments native to the land. One particular procedure that they were trained to do involved "attaching" their aura to the aura of the person being treated. This apparently resulted in a kind of X-ray vision that enabled the healer to "see" into the body and know what was wrong. The patient, in turn, was treated accordingly, with homeopathic-type remedies, as well as the use of chiropractic-type adjustment and even surgery.

It seems that the most unusual and esoteric of all the four initiates were those Albion referred to as the *KA Priests*. These special ones were portrayed in the artwork of the time as having blue skin. KA Priests were taught to safely enter the World of the Dead and to return. This esoteric art was a highly elaborate operation involving a connection with the dying one, usually one of high rank such as a pharaoh, queen, prince, or other initiate. The KA Priest, in consciousness, accompanied the soul of the dead to the Otherworld, even assisting him to adjust to the different state of reality that death brings. These men knew the realm of spirits as well as the physical world and traveled back and forth, at will, fulfilling the spiritual tasks for which they were trained.

Sound and light shows are performed every night at Karnak Temple. The program lasts for one and one-half hours and tells the story of ancient Thebes.

On the west bank of the Nile, across from Luxor, lies the Valley of the Kings and Queens. The area is a huge electrical grid, the location of many tombs of pharaohs and queens.

Valley of the Kings and Queens

Sixty-four tombs of pharaohs have been found in the Valley of the Kings, some of which are open to the public, including the tombs of King Tut, Amenhotep, Seti I, Ramses VI, Thutmose, and Ramses III.

In the nearby Valley of the Queens some fifty-seven tombs have been found. Not all are worth a visit or even open to the public, with the fabulous exception of the tomb of Nefertari, wife of Ramses II, most famous for its artwork. Special permission must be obtained for visiting this tomb as it is described as unsafe. The energy from the tombs can be experienced simply be being in the grid of the valley, and it is a good location for meditation and attunement to the land to "read" the history of the ancient past.

Since the sun descended into darkness in the west, the west bank of the Nile was considered the habitation of the dead. Within this area, known as the Valley of the Kings and Queens, are the burial grounds of the pharaohs, which can only be reached by ferry across the Nile from Luxor. Nestled in the nearby cliffs are the Tombs of the Nobles. The interior of these tombs, which are open to the public, are beautifully decorated with scenes of ancient Egyptian life. Inscriptions known as hieroglyphics tell the tales of the distant past, but they remain so vivid that one finds it difficult to believe that they are so old. Here, in lonely desolation, the powerful pharaohs were brought to rest. Tombs designed to keep them comfortable and safe failed miserably. Only the tomb of Tutankhamen still contains its owner's mummy. The mummy was returned after misfortune befell so many associated with the opening of the tomb. As a result, the artifacts may tour the world, but Tut remains in his tomb.

In 1881 a cache of royal mummies was discovered buried together at Dier el Bahri, the magnificent temple of Queen Hatshepsut. It appeared that they had been collected at some point in time and put there for safekeeping after their tombs had been ransacked. Hatshepsut's Temple is acknowledged as one of the most remarkably beautiful edifices surviving the centuries of Egyptian history. It awes, even in its incomplete restoration, which is currently an ongoing project. Thirty-four hundred years have not dimmed the painted walls in some of the elaborately decorated rooms!

Of course, Ramses II outdid everyone, even in death. His temple is the grandest of all. His life matched his monuments, with 150 children to mourn his passing, and the longest reign of any ruler in Egyptian history.

But not all the tombs in the Valley of the Kings were

built for rulers. The nobles who served their pharaohs are there, too. Their tombs give the most intimate glimpse into day-to-day life to be found anywhere. Ramose, vizier to Amenhotep III and his son, Akhenaten, began to create his eventual resting place in this valley, but was forced to abandon the project when Akhenaten moved the palace and temple complex to what is now known as el Amarna, far from Karnak. The wall decorations in this tomb reflect not only the changing political events, but the subtle changes in every aspect of life, including the style of art that was acceptable under the new pharaoh's insistence on complete "truth" in all things.

The giant statues known as the Collosi of Memnon are nearby, still gazing across the green fields toward the Nile. Since repair was done to preserve them, the odd humming noise that was created by the wind moving through the cracks in their stones is now absent.

Denderah:

North of Luxor, about forty miles, is Denderah. Accessible by train, hired taxi, or bus, this old capital of this sixth district of Upper Egypt is the site of the Temple of Hathor, one of the most wonderful and well-preserved temples in all Egypt. The temple, dedicated to Hathor, the goddess of joy and love, took over a hundred years to build. The elaborately decorated temple, although badly defaced by reported Christian zealots, is still lovely to behold. This is a strong electrical vortex. The really exciting features of this site are on the roof, where there are two rooms, or chapels. One contains a reproduction of the zodiac. Drawings of the last, and most famous, of the seven Cleopatras in Egypt can be seen on the back walls of the zodiac room.

Denderah was another place that got Albion's attention. Prior to our journey to the temple in 1987, a channeling was given that interested us all a great deal. He spoke of its having once been the place where young women were trained as *Star Priestesses*.

According to Albion, there were two places in which holy orders of women were quite prominent in Egypt, at different times and for different purposes. One, of course, was the Temple of Isis. The second one was the Temple of Denderah. This was not exclusively a women's temple, nor was it built exclusively for women's rites and ceremonies. There was, however, a small order of women at this temple, which never numbered more than seven at a time. Once a woman was accepted into this Order of the Goddess Nut, the only way her seat became vacated was through her death. So the old priestesses reigned supreme and solid for many years before there was a seat vacant.

There were basically seven stages of learning or initiation in the Order of the Goddess Nut. The society was not like those you may know where the student reads something someone has said and decides whether it is true. In those times, one had to experience it; one had to become the owner of the knowledge through experience. At one point during the stages of initiation, a priestess was supposed to see a comet as an omen. If she did not see the comet within seven years, she was considered unclean in her heart and put on probation for three years. If, by the end of the probationary period, the priestess still had not seen a comet, it was decided by a council of the six remaining priestesses whether or not that priestess should be put to death, for the order could not be contaminated with someone unclean in thought or heart.

Another vortex is fifty miles north of Denderah and is called Abydos. The temple, seven miles west of the Nile, is accessible by auto, donkey, or carriage. Abydos has long been a place of pilgrimage. Legend has it that the tomb of Osiris is located here, Osiris being the god of the Underworld and the husband of the goddess Isis. The wall drawings here are truly magnificent, and plenty of time should be allowed to enjoy them, along with the reliefs. There are seven sanctuaries here, each dedicated to a different deity.

Esna and Edfu:

South of Luxor some thirty miles is Esna, another vortex site. The Temple of Khnum there is Ptolemaic in origin, and long before that, was a site of worship. Forty miles farther south is Edfu, where there is a site that the ancient Greeks called Appollonopolis, after the god Apollo. Here one finds the Temple of Horus, well-preserved and beautifully artistic. Both temples at Esna and Edfu are electric in nature.

Aswan

Aswan is located 534 miles south of Cairo. Since its beginning, this city has been the trade route from Egypt to Central Africa. Today it is a rare combination of the influence of both its Oriental and African history. The current population is a whopping half million people. Its growth is primarily attributed to its being the site of the famous Aswan High Dam. Part of the charm of Aswan can be experienced by taking a ride in a felucca on the Nile. The felucca is the Egyptian Nile's taxi. Feluccas come in many sizes, but each graceful boat, with its tall, billowing sail, has the power to thrill the tourist in a unique experience. The crew may be a single, galabia-clad man of great age and wisdom, or a young lad who serenades his guests with a Nubian love song. A ride on the Nile at sunset makes time disappear, and the Nile's power becomes a key to the ancient past.

Aswan's climate is very dry. When I was there in the fall of 1987, it had rained for the first time in ten years! Our guide told us he had awakened his six-year-old daughter, taken her outside to see and feel the rain, and told her to remember it because it might be many years before she would have the experience again. Aswan has long been considered a winter resort because of its beauty and lush greenery.

Isle of Philae: One of the most intense vortices in Egypt, electromagnetic in nature, is located south of Aswan and easily reached by taxi and then by boat. The lovely Temple of Isis was discovered underwater in the Nile and moved to its present site from the Isle of Philae. Each time I have gone there, I have gotten the distinct impression that it had been a temple inhabited by women, perhaps for training into a holy order dedicated to worship and service of the goddess Isis, the Great Mother. I consider this to be a wonderful place for one to meditate and to get in closer touch with the feminine energies within oneself. The cult of Isis continued to reign on Philae long after the advent of Christianity during the Roman periods in the country. The entire island is an electromagnetic vortex, with the Holy of Holies altar as the vortex epicenter. There is a sound and light show at the Temple of Isis.

Temple of Abu Simbal: One finds the relocated site of the Temple of Abu Simbal 168 miles south of Aswan accessible by plane. This huge complex was built by Ramses II and dedicated to the three principal gods of ancient Egypt: Amen-Ra, Ptah, and Ha-Rakte, an aspect of the sun god, Horus. The feeling of solar ceremonies and solar energy pervade this site, which makes it a good place for recharging one's physical self and getting in touch with the High Self. Abu Simbal is highly electrical in its nature. Twice a year the sun's rays illumine the four statues on the farthest wall of the temple. These statues are of the three gods and Ramses II himself!

Its original location was the site of an electric ley terminal. A sacred spot, it is the site of two large temples built by Pharaoh Ramses II and his queen Nefertari. The temples have been moved for preservation purposes and can also be reached by plane. Flights are available out of Aswan or Luxor several times a day.

In 1964 UNICEF organized the removal of the temple, piece by piece, to higher ground, because the rising waters of Lake Nasser would have soon engulfed it. The temple was opened in its new location September 22, 1968.

Aswan Dam: The Aswan High Dam is a man-made grid area of concentrated magnetic energy from the Nile.

Tours of the dam are available. This site has created, according to Albion, a negative energy due to its adverse effects on the land and people. It has created Lake Nasser by holding back the waters that formerly flooded the land and revitalized the soil each year.

Egypt's lure is unmistakable. In some ways, the country has changed, and in other, more profoundly spiritual ways, it has not changed at all. It is truly a land of beginnings, a land whose roots go back to the very onset of civilization. The bountiful Nile, the antique monuments and temples, the lingering energies of the ancient gods and goddesses, and the intensity of the people all weave together to form one of the most mystical and mysterious sites on Mother Earth. Making a pilgrimage to Egypt is truly a quest of the heart.

CHAPTER SIX

TIBET:
Land Where Prayers
Never Cease

In the Himalayas of Nepal and Tibet a Buddhist chant is inscribed on prayer stones, prayer wheels, prayer flags, and even on the living rocks: OM MANI PADME HUM. Carried silently on the wind (so the Buddhists believe), the incantation spirals upward into the pure bright air above the radiant peaks of the highest mountains in the world. Translated literally, the chant goes like this: "Om! The jewel in the heart of the lotus. Hum!" Interpreted freely, it means, "the Truth within the unfolding world of phenomena, all change and all becoming."

The Blue Planet
LOUISE B. YOUNG

Tibetan History and Geography

"Tibet is a country of contradictions. . . . It is heaven and hell all in one place." These are the words of an American couple who led a pilgrimage to Tibet in October of 1986. For some time Joy and Jason Kuhn of Phoenix, Arizona, had felt a "mysterious calling" to go to Tibet, not really knowing why. What they experienced would forever change their perspective of Tibet, its people, and themselves.

TIBET

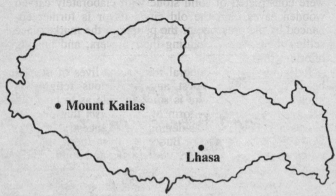

Tibet is one of the least populated places in the world. Covering an area of nearly a half million square miles, the country is home to almost two million people. The extreme altitude is a force to be reckoned with, most of the land mass being over fifteen thousand feet above sea level. The soil can grow only the heartiest of crops. Much of the rugged terrain is impassable in winter, when temperatures can drop as low as forty below due to biting winds and heavy snowfalls. The question surely arises: How can anyone live in this inhospitable land?

Despite the challenges it presents to human survival, Tibet is a country of awesome beauty. Located in the majestic Himalayan Mountains of Central Asia, it has often been called "the roof of the world." Its Earth gems include the world's highest peak. Known as Chomolungma to the locals, Mount Everest soars nearly six miles into the cold blue skies. With the snow-capped mountains and sacred peaks, there is little wonder why the people themselves have named their home the "Land of Snows."

Lhasa is the country's capital. About a two-hour drive from the airstrip where visitors first arrive, the ancient city is believed to be over fourteen centuries old. Today, Lhasa is actually composed of two distinct cities, one modern and one old. Most of the buildings in the old city were constructed of solid stone with elaborately carved wooden eaves, and the old city's flavor is further enhanced by the presence of the people in the marketplace selling their wares, chanting their prayers, and making offerings to their gods.

Religion plays an integral role in the lives of the Tibetan people. The oldest and indigenous religion is known as *Bon*, but there is some dispute as to how old it actually is. Bon is a form of *shamanism* that encompasses a belief in gods, demons, and ancestral spirits. However, with the rise of Buddhism from India, the two religions merged together, with each one adopting certain beliefs and practices of the other. The love of religion in the traditional peoples' lives is not simply a matter of occasional ritual and blind acceptance of a code of beliefs. Their religion is a deeply woven pattern in the fabric of their everyday lives. Traces of Bon, with its strong similarities to the Native American religious practices on the faraway North American continent, have left an ancient type of perspective in which rocks, rivers, mountains, and trees are considered to be the domain of spirits. As a result, Tibetans seek to honor such places with offerings and prayers whenever they come in contact with them.

Prayer is the tool of power and the greatest asset to come out of both Bon and Buddhism. The familiar prayer wheel is found everywhere and varies in size, from being small enough to be held in the hand to those found in the temples that are larger than a man. Printed prayers are sold by the millions. Similar to the *pahos* of the Hopi people or prayer sticks with feathers tied to one end, prayer flags decorated with multicolored cloths dot the landscape as tokens of the devout faith of the people.

To the Tibetans, the true reward of religion is the "connection" it brings between themselves and higher levels of consciousness. This higher plane attunement is believed to allow the people clearer communication among each other, as well as giving access to and communication with meditational deities called *yidams* of the

"other worlds." Being in touch with such a higher reality also serves to counteract such human faults as
vengefulness and malice.

Bon has left still another ingredient in the religious life
of the people that is reminiscent of the Native Americans. Both have shamans whose task it is to cure the sick,
exorcise evil spirits, speak for spirits, and communicate
with the dead. Even though Buddhism's monastic disciplines have gained supremacy in Tibet, this has not sup-
pressed the Bon-type practices amongst the traditional
peoples.

The Tibet of today is a troubled country, both politi-
cally and spiritually. Since the Chinese invasion and an-
nexation of the country in 1951, an attempt has been made
to eliminate the strong influence of religion from the lives
of the Tibetan faithful. Under Chinese administration,
the country lies largely hidden from the rest of the world,
plagued by frequent civil uprisings against the Chinese
domination. It is estimated that over two-hundred-
thousand Tibetans fled the land, along with the Dalai
Lama, due to China's threat and influence. Tibet is rapidly losing the uniqueness that it once possessed. It is no
longer a country that is stable, peaceful, and harmonious
according to the Buddhist tradition. With the Dalai Lama
in exile, the Tibetan people are "cut off" from their spiritual leader, and the sanctuary he provides and represents
for the practice of their unique version of Buddhism.
Since occupying the country, the Chinese have turned a
deaf ear to the voices of the Tibetans. There continue to
be uprisings and setbacks in the actions Tibetans have
taken to win their deserved independence. The Dalai
Lama's policy of peace and compassion has, thus far,
brought little change or progress in the current state of
affairs. The battle of the Tibetans, so it seems, is a losing
one, but it goes on. Perhaps the Dalai Lama's winning
of the Nobel Peace Prize in 1989 will eventually lead to
the ears and eyes of the world being focused on Tibet's
plight and the social, political, and spiritual injustices
that these people are suffering.

The Dalai Lama, the spiritual and political leader of

the Tibetan people, is unique in the world, possessing a
title of rulership for over five hundred years. To date,
fourteen Dalai Lamas have ruled in succession, each believed to be a reincarnation of the other. All Dalai Lamas
are considered to be incarnations of Chenrezi, Bodhisattva of Divine Compassion. Although presently in exile, the current Dalai Lama still has a powerful hold on
the spiritual consciousness of the people. Perhaps to help
make the plight of the country and its people known, the
spiritual leader and some of his lama priests have come
to the West to teach the dharma. As a result, teaching
centers have been established throughout the United
States and Europe to spread the intriguing form of Tibetan Buddhism. It is interesting to note that some lamas
have recently met with elders and spokespersons of the
Native Americans in the American Southwest, namely
the Hopi. Both cultures are united by the threat of the
loss of their traditional ways.

Tibetan Book of the Dead

Behind the prayer wheels and flags, religious images,
chants, and other esoteric practices of the people exists
the very essence of Tibetan spirituality. This essence
manifests as a complex web of commentary on the processes of birth, life, death, and rebirth known as *sam-
sara*. The Tibetan Book of the Dead, one of the sacred
scriptures of the people, is a book about the cycle of
death and rebirth. It tells of a soul's journey from one
life to another, giving the Seeker wise advice about how
to learn from one's past and present errors as well as of
the importance of, and how to discern and perfect, one's
destiny. True to all eastern teachings, the Doctrine of
Reincarnation is an integral part of Tibetan philosophy.
It teaches constant rebirth. In fact, according to its scriptures, life is but a "testing ground" for the soul in its
long, arduous task of returning to the One Source, the
Creator.

Tibetans rely upon an ancient way of "knowing": in-

tuition. The intuitive revelations of various Tibetan and
Indian sages and gurus, including the Buddha himself,
have been recorded in the Book of the Dead, forming
one of the oldest, and most unique, religious systems
known to man.

From the Tibetan perspective, all life revolves around
the Law of Karma. This central doctrine teaches that all
actions, or *karmas*, have consequences, which is why
this doctrine is often referred to as the Law of Cause and
Effect. Some actions, so it is taught, must be paid for or
are rewarded immediately, while others are repaid or rewarded later in the same or even a future lifetime. A
quote from the Tibetan Book of the Dead states: "Without some after-death resolution of actions, the principle
of cause and effect becomes meaningless." And so the
Tibetans believe that good deeds during life help one to
accumulate "merit" or good karma, which is the goal of
all actions.

Tibetans have a specific attitude about death. Preparation for death is as important as living. Death prepares
one for rebirth, as it is a time of "processing" one's
previous earthly experiences. The realm within which this
processing takes place is called the *bardo*. Death and
life, two states that are inextricably entwined into a complex symphony of evolutionary progress. Death prepares
one for rebirth, as it is a time of "processing" one's
previous earthly experiences. The realm within which this
processing takes place is called the bardo. Viewed from
this perspective, death and life are states, both of which
are necessary parts of the evolutionary cycle.

When leafing through the Tibetan Book of the Dead, I
came across a most intriguing segment of information
that concerned what was called "A Traveler's Guide to
Other Worlds." I realized that I had come across an intriguing part of Tibetan religion. The commentary involves the religious perspective of how the location of
one's birth affects one's life. In a particular section of the
doctrine entitled "The Choosing of the Womb-Door,"
instructions are given for the soul who is preparing to
incarnate. They concern the selection of a body or ve-

hicle and opportunity for the next birth. Instructions are given to the deceased, whose name is spoken aloud three times. The deceased is then encouraged to know it will soon be time to be reborn and to make a selection of the right place (womb) for that rebirth. The proper "Continent" is also included in the place chosen. However, when the so-called Continents themselves are carefully studied, you realize that the "Continents" are not just Earth continents, but places in the "Outer Ocean of Space," of which the Earth is but one! This seems to suggest that the Tibetans believe that the Earth is not the only inhabitable or inhabited planet in the universe and that the physical realm is not the only dimension of existence.

I also learned that there are four major Continents, situated in the four directions. Lupah, the Vast Body, is the eastern one. Existence there is one of tranquil-mindedness and virtue. However, the deceased is advised against going to Lupah, for even though it is a place of ease, there is no religion there to speak of. Jambuling, or Jambu, the Southern Continent, is the planet Earth and is said to be the smallest of the four. It is a place of delightful mansions, where riches and plenty abound. This is the place the deceased is advised to enter.

The third continent, Palengchod, the western one, is a powerful place, where the people are extremely strong and where cattle is eaten as the main food. This place is also advised against, for religion does not prevail there. The Northern Continent, known as Daminyan, is the largest of the four. In this place, trees grow in abundance and supply all the wants and needs of those incarnated there. This is a place of long life and merit but also has no religion, which is undesirable. We can see from this that the Earth is *the* desirable place to live to the Tibetans and that the other three are considered undesirable, primarily due to the weakness or absence of religion.

Aside from the four main Continents, there are eight "satellite" Continents, one being on either side of the major four. These satellite Continents resemble the Continents to which they are attached but are about half their

size. For example, the left satellite to the Earth is the
place where Padma Sambhava, the Great Guru of La-
maism, is said to have gone to teach goodness and salvation and now reigns there as a king. The descriptions
of the four main Continents where the deceased may be
reborn contain highly symbolic "visions" of errors and
indulgences to be recognized and avoided.

The presence of *religion* is the one deciding and pertinent factor involved in the deceased making the proper
choice of rebirth. From the Book of the Dead, "choose
that in which religion prevailed and enter therein." It is
also pointed out that in selecting a "womb-door," there
is room for error. "Through the influence of *karma*, good
wombs may appear bad and bad wombs may appear
good." The key to choosing is to be free of any attraction to the good, and revulsion to the bad. Freeing oneself of attraction and revulsion is to be impartial, which
is considered to be the most profound of the spiritual
arts. The preferable address is repeated to the deceased
seven times and he is encouraged to get upon, and stay
upon, the Yellow Light Path of human beings. Human
birth is considered rare by Tibetan Buddhists. It is a
"precious" opportunity that must be honored and taken
full advantage of by right living. Otherwise, one can be
reborn as an animal, hungry ghost, hell being, or other
lower and inferior entity who has no hope of attaining
Enlightenment.

Buddhism

There are three trends of Indian Buddhism that have
been integrated into Tibetan Buddhism. The first is *Hi-
nayana*, which represents the basic teachings of the historical Buddha and is the lesser vehicle to Enlightenment.
Mahayana is the second. It introduces the further evolution of ethical and philosophical understanding that
started to emerge in India about five hundred years after
Skakyamuni and is the "greater vehicle." It asks that
one renounce any further involvement in the plight of the

world and strive for his own release in the unconditional realm of Nirvana. It is founded on detachment and release as well as Love and Compassion. The ideal is the *boddhisatva*, the person who selflessly aspires to release Enlightenment for the sake of all that lives. *Vajrayana*, the third trend, is the culmination of the other two traditions. It is a powerful, direct path that utilizes symbolic imagination, mantric sound, and subtle physical energy to effect a complete psycho-physical transformation.

Mantras are also an integral part of Tibetan spirituality. A mantra appears in the opening quote to this Chapter, Om Mani Padme Hum. When spoken properly, a mantra invokes the supreme power of sound that corresponds to a particular rate of vibration of high spiritual beings and forces. Because of their power, mantras are carefully guarded. There are special lines of gurus who are solely entrusted with this guardianship and are known as the Brotherhood of Guardians of the Mysteries. Such lamas are well tested before the mysteries are given to them for safekeeping and practice. Mantras invoke the powers of the various male and female deities. When a mantra is uttered, the spiritual force involved is awakened and comes, on command, to the initiate. The mantra taught to the initiate is one to invoke the Goddess Kundalini. Depending upon the wise or foolish use of that mantra, the guru will soon know, for the Awakened One can destroy as well as save. Also, unless the other mantras are toned properly, they are without effect. When seen in writing by the uninitiated, the prayers are meaningless. The correct pronunciation of a mantra of a deity depends upon body purity as well as upon proper intonation. Therefore, a devotee must first work with a purification mantra. The mouth and tongue are purified, and then the actions themselves. This process is said to give life to, or awaken, the "sleeping power" of the mantra. To be capable of correctly employing these sounds confers supernatural powers, called Siddhi, which can be used for good or evil, depending totally upon the character of the guru. The good path leads to Emancipation, while the evil path leads to Enslavement.

Joy Kuhn was struck by the friendliness of the Tibetan people as well as "their obvious religious devotion." "However," she commented, "there was something in their eyes . . . a deep sadness . . . an anger . . . a hatred for the Chinese and the devastation brought to their land and their way of life." Despite the obvious repression, the Kuhns and their entourage remarked on the people's love of life and their awareness and honor of the spiritual forces with which they seek to achieve a harmonious balance. Their natural sense of humor was evidenced in the twinkling of their eyes and the laugh lines that were etched on their faces. "They have their prayer beads in hand and are going at it [prayer] all the time . . . and chanting." As the Kuhns talked about the land and its people, their experiences began to give me a good idea of this unique place. "(The land) is very pretty. . . . Snow-capped mountains are all around . . . huge valleys . . . clouds, everywhere clouds meet mountains and monasteries. Tibet, we felt, is a masculine energy . . . alive . . . very earthy. Everywhere there are plowed fields. These people are close to the Earth . . . they depend totally on the Earth for survival. The days were cool, the nights were cold . . . no rain, just the ever-present clouds.

"They (Tibetans) liked us. They like westerners. They are so religious. But you can sense their anger. There is a strong military presence . . . the Chinese. They do have uprisings . . . it's like a powder keg all the time. All the lamas who had the high spiritual knowledge have left. The ones that remain that have the true high knowledge are few. We had audience with an old lama. . . . He seemed bored . . . he mostly continued to read his newspaper."

"There are no wealthy Tibetans. There is a feeling of being confined that we sensed from them." When asked to sum up their feelings about the country and the people, Jason replied: "Poignant." Joy said, thoughtfully: "The country has been spiritually raped, and so have the people."

All through our conversation, the Kuhns kept referring

again and again to the mountains. "Ah, the energy of those mountains . . . and, at night, more stars than one can describe."

The Himalayan Mountains are the companions of the people. In geological terms, they are a young range, originating some four million years ago. When tectonic plate movement caused India to slam into the soft underside of Asia, the terrain was pushed skyward. The mountains are still rising at the startling rate of several inches a year! What was once a lush and fertile place is now one of the most harsh and life-defying areas on Earth. Basically, Tibet has three different geographical regions: the huge Northern Plateau, the Outer Plateau in the West, and the Southeastern Plateau in the Southeast. The climate of the Northern Plateau is one of the worst in the world, with strong winds and extremely cold temperatures. There is salt in the soil, and little rainfall, making crop growth and general plant life extremely limited and difficult. Likewise, many animal species are impoverished due to the high altitudes and climatic conditions. The adaptable yak is the one hero, providing transport, food, and companionship under the awful stress of life in the Tibetan wastelands.

Mount Kailas

Among the multitude of snow-covered Himalayan peaks lies Mount Kailas. Small as mountains go in this area, Mount Kailas, 6,714 feet high, is a sacred mountain. This powerful electrical vortex has been called "the soul of the country" and is believed to protect the people and assure survival. A unique natural feature of the mountain is that four of the largest rivers in Asia have their sources within sixty miles of it: the Brahmaputra, Karnali, Ganges, and the Sutlej. Hindus consider Kailas to be the throne of Shiva, the god of destruction and reproduction who forms the supreme triad with Brahma and Vishnu. The ancient religion, Bon, also revered it as being the place where their founder, Shenrab, came down

to Earth from the sky. The pilgrimage route around the
mountain starts near the main road and takes two to three
days to complete. Pilgrims have been going to Mount
Kailas for over two thousand years, seeing it, walking
around it, and ascending it for meditation and prayer.
Closed to pilgrims for many years at the time of the Chinese invasion, the mountain has been reopened only to
Tibetan and Indian devotees since 1984. Visitors must
keep in mind that the area is quite difficult to reach. Stories abound regarding the magical powers of the mountain, powers that have been known to put severe obstacles
in the path of would-be pilgrims. Also, only those who
possess sufficient spiritual energy and who have made
appropriate preparations are allowed a glimpse of its sacred presence.

The religion of Tibet is far more complex than I am
able to fully understand and/or portray in a capsulized
manner here. However, I have concluded that the most
fundamental teachings may be summed up as follows:

• All possible realms of existence and states are entirely dependent upon phenomena.
• All phenomena are illusory and exist only in the
mind that perceives them.
• In Reality there are no gods, demons, spirits, or sen-
tient creatures, for all are illusory, therefore dependent
upon a "cause."
• Cause is a yearning after sensation and unstable existence.
• Rebirth is a fact.
• After-death existence is but a continuation of the
phenomena-born existence of the human world, and both
states are karmic.
• The nature of existence intervening between death
and rebirth is determined by antecedent actions. This is
a psychological dreamlike state resulting from the mind
content of the percipient.
• Rebirth continues until Enlightenment is achieved.
Enlightenment results in the realization of the unreality
of existence.

- Controlling the thinking processes is essential and is called *yoga*.
- One needs a human guru.
- The greatest guru is Gautama the Buddha. Lesser spiritually aware beings can bestow grace, though they themselves are not freed from illusion.
- The goal of spiritual freedom is *Nirvana*, which is beyond all paradises and all hells.
- Nirvana is the ending of all sorrow.
- And, finally, Nirvana *is* Reality.

The mantra Om Mani Padme Hum (pronounced OM MANEE PAYMAY HUNG by Tibetans) has been called "the melody of Tibet." It is repeated constantly by the faithful as they move their prayer beads, one by one, through their fingers . . . counting . . . ever counting to earn merit. The mantra serves the purpose of helping the praying one to concentrate upon the prayers as well as upon the meaning of compassion, which the holy sounds stir in the heart and is a devotion to Chenrezi. The ideal of this devotion is the *Bodhisattva* consciousness. The Bodhisattva is one who is selfless and who aspires to Enlightenment for the good of all that exists. This compassion is symbolized by syllables carved on rocks around holy shrines, on walls of the temples, doors, and even etched on the hillsides around cities and villages everywhere.

Lama is a term used to mean *guru* or spiritual teacher. In Tibetan religion, the lama plays the important role of instructor, and the student must devote himself fully to his teachings. Of course, the most well-known lama of them all is the Dalai Lama himself.

Sacred Sites

Because Tibet is a country that revolves around religion, it is a land filled with Sacred Sites and, due to the terrain, natural Earth vortices. The entire country of Tibet is an electrical grid. Because of the sheer number of such places, I have made a careful effort to point out the most notable of the Sacred Sites. Also, I have concluded the whereabouts of the natural power spots and come to realize that many of these locations qualify as both Sacred Sites and as natural vortices. Some of the sites mentioned are given in their phonetic spelling, as per my informants' knowledge and understanding.

Lhasa

Lhasa is a natural electrical vortex, although the city itself has grown far beyond the bounds of the vortex, which is centered in the western part of the city and is the site of the revered Potala, a potent sacred palace. Called the Red Palace, the Potala sits atop the "Red Hill" that dominates Lhasa. It dates back to 1645, and its construction was completed in 1694. The palace is named after Mount Potala in India, a sacred peak to the Hindu god Shiva, and has served as home to the successive Dalai Lamas and their staffs since the era of the Fifth until the present. A minimum entrance fee is charged, and the palace is open to the public every day except Sunday.

A hill located just in front of the Potala is called Chak Phuri. Translated to mean "Iron Mountain," this is a Sacred Site and a part of the large natural vortex of the area. I have been informed by the guru of a close friend, Lama Karma Rinchen, who now lives in Hawaii, that it is a place where rituals have long been done. Chak Phuri Hill is called Medicine King Hill and is one of central Tibet's four holy mountains, and the only one near Lhasa. The holy mountains are considered to be the soul of the country. The founder of Tibetan medicine lived on Chak Phuri during the reign of King Gampo.

On the south side of Lhasa, also according to Lama Karma Rinchen, is located what may well be one of the few magnetic power spots in Tibet. Called Tsa Ri, this sacred mountain is open every thirteen years to pilgrims to allow for certain rituals to take place. At other times the people are allowed to journey to the middle of the mountain, which is lush with tropical vegetation, for the purpose of purification. On top of the mountain is a crystal stupa, an ancient man-built structure, designed to amplify the natural energy that is present. I am certain this magnetic vortex site aids in the inner cleansing process, as all such vortices would.

While on the subject of magnetic vortices, I must mention two lakes: Manasarovar and Rakshas Tal. Located south of Mount Kailas, in western Tibet, at the base of Mount Gurla Mandhata, these two small vortices are the highest freshwater lakes in the world. It is believed that when the waters are flowing in the channel that connects the two bodies of water, it is a good sign of fortune for the Tibetan people. Manasarovar, the larger of the two, is believed to be the place where the Buddha's mother was carried by the gods to be washed prior to giving birth to the Buddha.

Another of the sacred mountains and natural electrical vortices of Tibet is Gangpo Ri. Located in an area south of Lhasa on the banks of the Brahmaputra River, this mountain is said to be the place where Avalokiteshvara descended to the land in the form of a monkey who coupled with a female demon to produce the first member of the Tibetan race. In addition to Mount Kailas and Mount Gangpo Ri, the third sacred mountain of Tibet is Hepori. As is true with most sacred peaks, Hepori is the site of a monastery, Samye. In ancient times, the king, Trisong Detsen, was said to have had his palace here. There is a mantra carved on a boulder on this mountain. Hepori is an electrical vortex and has long been the site where the first Tibetans were ordained as monks. This, subsequently, is a place where one could go specifically for the purpose of "awakening" the soul within. The fourth and final sacred mountain of Tibet is located in Gongkar, about sixty miles south of Lhasa. Called Chuwori, the area is the site of an old castle, Gongkar Dzong, which now is in ruins.

I have been told that in the eastern part of the country, there is a Sacred Site called Tsa Dra Rinchen Trak, which translates to mean "very great similar precious cliff," which is the location of the Plapung Monastery. Every twelve years, in the Sheep Year, the site is open to pilgrims.

Also near Lhasa is To Lung Tsurpo, the mountain location where the Tsurpo Monastery was built. The name means "Ocean of Tranquillity." It is known by the people as Chakrasambhara's Place, who was one of the most potent of deities, namely a "protector."

Again we must go to eastern Tibet, where we find Tsa Warong Khawha Karpo or "Hot Valley Snow Mountain." According to my sources, this is a great secret place that is only open once a year to pilgrims. Local inquiry is the only means of obtaining further information about this place.

Monasteries and Temples

The monasteries in Tibet are numerous. Each is a Sacred Site and is built in a location where the Earth energy is an especially powerful vortex or grid, usually electrical in charge. The following is a comprehensive list of some of the major monasteries, with their general locations:

Jokhang: Called the most sacred temple in Tibet, Jokhang is located in the old city of Lhasa.

The Potala: Located at the west of the city of Lhasa.

The Norbulingka: Located just west of Lhasa. This is called the People's Park.

Sera Monastery: Located north of Lhasa, Sera was once a place of monastic training.

Drepung Monastery: Located west of Lhasa.

Nechung Monastery: Located very close to the Drepung Monastery.

Ramoche Temple: Lhasa.

Gyu-me: Lhasa.

Palhalupuk Temple: Located in Lhasa, Palhalupuk is quite magnetic and is formed from a cave at the base of

Chakpori Hill. The temple is open all day and there is no admission charge.

Ganden Monastery: Located about 24 miles east of Lhasa, Ganden is in ruins, for the most part.

Yerpa: This is also an electromagnetic energy site and is located in central Tibet some thirty kilometers northeast of Lhasa.

Reting Monastery: One hundred kilometers north of Lhasa, Reting is an electromagnetic site and is located in a juniper forest.

Trandruk Temple: Located about seven kilometers south of Tsetang, Trandruk is considered to be one of the first Buddhist temples in Tibet.

Yumbulagang: Located just south of Tsetang, it is currently a chapel.

Drongtse Monastery: Located just outside of Gyantse.

Tashilhunpo Monastery: Located on the western end of the city of Shigatse.

The Kumbum: This is a spectacular stupa temple whose name means "Place of a Thousand Images." It is the largest stupa in Tibet and was built in 1927 by a prince of Gyantse.

Tsurphu: This monastery was founded by the first Karmapa. It is the most important place for the Karmapa sect. The ruins are impressive. It is located forty kilometers from Lhasa, northward on the main road toward Yangbaling. Turn left (west) off the road, cross the bridge, and continue for another thirty kilometers.

Tara's Mountain: This is the site of a monastery located on the west side of Shigatse. The monastery, Tashilhunpo, was founded in 1447. It is one of Tibet's most active monasteries. Tashilhunpo is open from 9:00 A.M. to noon, and there is a small admission fee.

Other interesting Sacred Sites in Tibet include:

Palalubu Temple: This is a small, ancient cave just off the main road in front of the Potala. It encloses a cave built by King Gampo's wives.

Valley of the Kings: These eight large mounds of earth

resembling natural hills are believed to contain the tombs of Tibet's later kings. The valley is sixteen miles south of Tse-dang. The kings were all warriors. It is located southeast of Lhasa in a large region of which Tsedang is the capital.

Mount Gongbori: This is one of central Tibet's holy mountains where a saintly monkey gave birth to the Tibetan people.

Milrepa's Cave: Milrepa is the Tibetan Saint Francis, the favorite of the people. He left a legacy of songs and poems, for he was a poet, an eccentric, a hermit, saint, and magician, possessing great occult powers. His image is smiling, with a hand to his ear. This cave is where he spent many years of his life and is located six miles north of Nyalann between the main road and the river in a tiny village called Zhonggang. Offerings appropriate to bring to this site include decorated stones or wildflowers and herbs.

There are so many monasteries to see in Tibet that trusting your intuition about which ones to visit is probably the best guidance to follow. For example, it was at the Samye Monastery that Joy Kuhn was able to "see" and "feel" what she said was a "spiral-like energy" emanating from the natural mountain upon which the monastery was erected. Any traveler to Tibet should be aware that any itinerary must be approved, prior to departure, by the Chinese government. A qualified travel agency should be able to help you get the necessary approval.

Based upon their experiences, the Kuhns felt it would also be helpful for the visitor to Tibet to remember that the extremely high altitude can be a physical problem. Oxygen is provided in some hotels, but the best plan is to not overdo and to allow ample time for adjustment, which, for the average person, is about three days. Headaches and nausea are common symptoms of altitude difficulties. Tibetan cuisine includes vegetables, fruits, meats, and soups. To be safe, Joy recommends that visitors take bouillon cubes and tea bags, both for nourishment and familiar tastes. The water in Tibet is unfit for drinking, and there is no system for purification. Bottled water can be purchased, or local water may be boiled for consumption.

Most of the monasteries in Tibet are isolated, up the sides of valleys, and difficult to reach. The Tibetan roads are generally poor, with little traffic. In addition to altitude sickness, travelers must also be prepared to shield themselves from exposure. It is safer to travel by bus or hired car in this country. Accommodations are rare, so it is recommended that travelers carry sleeping bags. It is important in Tibet that travelers give themselves plenty of time to travel and enjoy the places they wish to see.

A journey to the Land of the Snows is a journey to the heart of the people who live there. It is truly a magical and mystical kingdom . . . isolated, troubled, majestic, and proud. Tibet is opening, albeit slowly, once again to visitors. Some religious practices are being allowed to be reborn, some temples and monasteries restored. One can see and experience what the country was and what it now has become, and in doing so, perhaps, get a feeling for its future. My feelings for this place were best summed up by Joy and Jason Kuhn's answer to my final question to them at the time of our interview:

Question: Did you enjoy your journey to Tibet?

Answer: "Yes . . . yes, we did. But it would have been so wonderful to have gone there at a time when the prayers never had ceased."

Since the time I began writing this chapter, a most profound event has occurred in my life. During a working visit to Hawaii in February 1989, I met, in person, Lama Karma Rinchen, head of the Kagyu Thegchen Ling Center of Tibetan Buddhism on Oahu. After much thought, I received Lama Rinchen as my "root lama" and took Refuge Vows, giving me the right and honor of becoming a Tibetan Buddhist. Guru and student practitioner are doing fine.

The Universe is just, and all its laws are kind and good. What we have earned comes upon us. We cannot question a wisdom that is beyond our understanding. The buddhas know best.

TIBETAN DEVOTEE

CHAPTER SEVEN

ENGLAND:
Ancient Druid Rocky Shore

> And did those feet in ancient times
> Walk upon England's mountains green;
> And was the holy Lamb of God,
> On England's pleasant pastures seen?
>
> WILLIAM BLAKE

English History and Geography

England is a sacred land. One of the most densely populated countries in the world, there is no place in England that is more than seventy-five miles from the sea. Within this tiny area has occurred a geological history of remarkable diversity that spans some six hundred million years. There was a time when large parts of central and southern England were submerged beneath warm seas. Now chains of low hills, built from sedimentary rock that was lifted and folded during primeval times, form nicely rounded hills and plateaus, sculpted by the great glaciers of three successive ice ages. When the ice melted, the landscape was changed further by deep deposits of glacial mud, sand, and gravel. In more modern times erosion brought about by rain, rivers, and the tides has continued to design the rolling hills and coastline.

The variety in the English landscape ranges from clay

ENGLAND

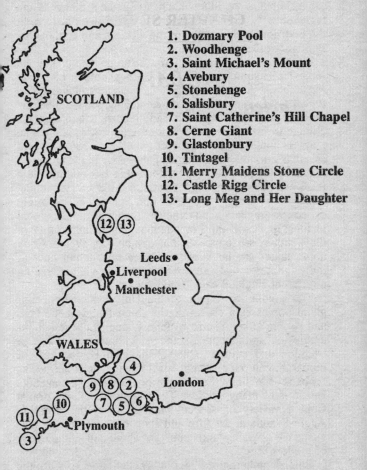

1. Dozmary Pool
2. Woodhenge
3. Saint Michael's Mount
4. Avebury
5. Stonehenge
6. Salisbury
7. Saint Catherine's Hill Chapel
8. Cerne Giant
9. Glastonbury
10. Tintagel
11. Merry Maidens Stone Circle
12. Castle Rigg Circle
13. Long Meg and Her Daughter

to sand, limestone to sandstone, chalk downs to alluvial river valleys. It is impossible to drive even short distances without seeing evidence of this geological complexity, particularly striking along the approximately two thousand miles of indented coastal areas. The beautiful quality of English scenery is owed to its geology. For example, local building materials in the Cotswolds are taken entirely from the terrain, to which we must credit the traditional appearance of the villages and settlements throughout the countryside.

England was separated from Europe by geological forces, and soon after the last Ice Age, much of it was swept bare. As a result of this, and the toll the dense population takes on the environment, England has a below-average range of vegetation and creature life. England's climate is one of the most erratic in the world, and it also plays an integral role in shaping the land. Temperatures can soar into the high nineties Fahrenheit in the summer, and to below zero degrees Fahrenheit in the winter. There is always snow in the higher parts of the country. Annual rainfall can vary, but it doesn't rain as much as one might expect, averaging twenty inches a year in the Southeast to forty inches in the low country. The changeability of the weather, season to season, day by day, even hour by hour, causes the landscape to dance in different hues of light and color that, no doubt, results in visitors seeing a different England each time they go.

The predominant part of the United Kingdom, England possesses a charm that is to be found in the land and people alike. The royal family, one of the few monarchies left in the world, is the very foundation of British tradition and culture. Queen Elizabeth II, the current monarch, can trace her ancestral lineage, so it is said, as far back as William the Conqueror. However, the average Briton is of many origins. Their language is also drawn from a variety of sources, mainly from the invading Anglo-Saxons in the fifth and sixth centuries. Their language has prevailed and counts for about half of the words of modern English.

English government is run by Parliament, with the monarch being little more than an official figurehead. The religion of the country is secular, the Church of England comprising the main religious body, with some eighteen thousand churches countrywide. Formed during a bitter dispute with the Catholic Church during the reign of Henry VIII, the Church of England shares the stage with about four million proclaimed Catholics and nonconformist Free Churches.

No one really knows who the original English people were or where they came from. According to some archaeological accounts, the land may have been inhabited well over a half million years ago, but the population was driven out by each succeeding ice age. It is also believed that the land has been continuously inhabited for the last ten thousand years, the time that marked the end of the last of the glaciers. If so, the occupants would have been mostly nomadic.

Mystical England

We know from historical records that those who lived in England in early times were a spiritually minded people, with Nature itself serving as their cathedrals, and natural phenomena embodying their gods and goddesses. In his book *The Traveler's Key to Sacred England*, famed English author John Mitchell writes about the nomads: "The paths they took, the places where they stopped, and the locations of episodes on their journey form the sacred geography of the nomads, who ritually imitate the actions of the creative spirits at the appropriate spots." There can be little doubt that a spiritual relationship existed between the land and the people.

Perhaps it was the Celts and the earlier middle Stone Age peoples to whom we owe the greatest debt regarding the precepts of the Old Religion that united man and his environment. Literally all aspects of life were celebrated. The people were connected to the Earth. Their land was dotted with the haunts of familiar spirits and linked together by a course of pathways upon which they traveled for celebration, ceremony, and spiritual pilgrimages. As the nomadic life came to a close and settlements cropped up, agriculture began. Along with it arose a whole new set of deities whose charge it was to insure good crops, protect the hamlet, and bestow good fortune.

Settlements also marked another wonderfully mysterious time in ancient Britain as well as in other places, namely the western coasts of Europe, the Canary Islands, Spain, Portugal, and parts of Scandinavia. Strange, sometimes huge, stone circles began to appear. It is apparent that the stone circles, of which there are over nine hundred that survive in England alone, were planned and built with geometric precision. Stonehenge, standing mute and gray on the Salisbury Plains in Wiltshire, is the most famous of all the megalithic sites in the world.

From my study of the science of astronomy, especially that of the ancient peoples of the world, I believe that the perspective presented in Gerald Hawkins's celebrated book *Stonehenge Decoded*, although not complete, is fact. Hawkins theorizes an astronomical usage of that specific stone circle. In short, Stonehenge was a calendar. A need for marking time, coupled with the possible honor bestowed upon certain phases of the Sun, Moon, constellations, and/or single stars, would have motivated ancient man to have cultivated an interest, perhaps more sophisticated than suspected, in his knowledge of the heavens. The currently developing new science of archaeoastronomy, which combines archeology and astronomy into one science for the purpose of investigating ancient sites, worldwide, is becoming a fine tool for unraveling the mysteries that time has erased from our view.

I feel, however, that stone circles were much more than calendrical in nature and purpose. The circles I have visited in Great Britain have a definite spiritual vibration, and I know intuitively that they were used for ritual and ceremony. It could be that what occurred there were ceremonies of initiations, celebrations of the seasons, invoking of celestial and Earth-based natural energies, and rituals to foretell the future or other forms of divination.

Geomancy

This is a good place to take into consideration an ancestral science that embodies the Earth wisdom and connections with Nature that I have based our fundamental thoughts and ideas upon since the onset of this writing. I refer, of course, to *geomancy*. Geomancy is defined by expert and author on the subject Nigel Pennick in *The Ancient Science of Geomancy*. "The science of putting human habitats and activities into harmony with the visible and invisible world around us was at one time universal, and vestiges of it remain in the landscape, architecture, ritual, and folklore of almost all countries in the world." Perhaps the wandering peoples of many ancient lands were indeed the authors of geomancy, but theories have been proposed that would place its origins back into eras that we refer to as Atlantean. When a question leads us as far back in time as the megalithic sites in Britain, we find that what the people of the time knew, who they were, and what their lives and religions consisted of, and how that religion was practiced, is sketchy, at best. I think that intuition must be relied upon and coupled with the few known facts based on archaeological evidence. It is then that a clear image begins to emerge. Unfortunately, as of yet, intuition is rarely regarded as an acceptable source of information in the face of science and its rules. At any rate, that has not stopped intuitive speculation on the part of individuals who are interested in pursuing the dim past of our ancestors and their way of life.

The very existence of geomancy tells us that what we have come to believe about ancient man is true: he understood and used the energies of the Earth. This was, no doubt, due to the fact that our forebears were directly dependent on the land and its powers for survival. Anything that important would certainly be held in sacred esteem. Another pertinent bit of knowledge concerning geomancy is that by and in its practice, Reality was viewed as a continuum within which everything was linked together, albeit in a subtle, often intangible manner. If one thinks about it, such a view does not allow for error, for error would inevitably upset the balance of it all. For example, in Feng Shui, the placing of a building in the wrong spot or facing the wrong way would result in dire consequences. For a Native American lodge used for ceremonial or dwelling purposes, to have an opening to the west rather than the traditional eastern direction would have been unthinkable. In their thinking, it would expose them to death instead of the life-giving powers of the rising Sun. Cosmic order must be kept at all costs.

Evidence shows us that the primitive people constructed or placed elaborate stone circles, medicine wheels, and single standing stones to mark special places and to serve as locations of worship and ritual. However, with the advent of Christianity, such practices, and more often than not, even the actual places themselves, were perceived as evil, and were thought to be inhabited by witches or other types of malefic spirits. Consequently these were often the very places upon which churches and monasteries were constructed to overcome and banish the negative influences and entities. From one perspective, this stirs resentment in the minds of many, for these structures severely damaged, and some even destroyed, the ancient sites. On the other hand, such Christian buildings, many of them built in the name of Saint Michael, who was the destroyer of pagan energies, do mark the locations of the sites themselves.

Ley Lines

One of the best known examples of this is the famous Saint Michael's (ley) Line in England. Beginning with Saint Michael's Mount, an eleventh-century monastery located off the coast of Cornwall near Land's End, the ley is said to run in a straight line through the Tor in Glastonbury. The Tor, another holy hill, the site of the ancient Avalon, is a five-hundred-foot natural mound that was man-terraced in pre-Arthurian times and believed to have been used as a place of Druid ritual. From Glastonbury, Saint Michael's Line passes through the Avebury henge, the site of the largest stone circle complex in Europe, and on through Stonehenge. Along the way, the ley also passes through a site of several ritual monuments on Bodwin Moor in Cornwall. It is curious to note that many of the major sites along the Saint Michael's Line, as well as in other areas of Britain and Europe, are natural mounds. Hills or mountains have long been not only the sites of pilgrimages and/or the ascent of heroes and spiritual leaders, but they have also been considered ideal places for man to communicate with the gods. Nigel Pennick states: "Almost every religion on Earth has its own holy mountain, and smaller versions may be found in most districts." The most famous example of this is found in Mount Olympus, holy mountain and home of the gods of ancient Greece. Man went to the mountain in order to be on high ground, above all else, no doubt a symbol and an act of human need and desire for reaching the abode of the gods and goddesses and supremacy. Holy hills are often vortices of Earth force and therefore sacred.

Whether one considers the Sacred Sites of our pagan ancestors, vortices, grids, or powerful ley line systems, England is the richest land on Earth for the Seeker. The British Isles are totally magnetic lands. Their island location, the terrain, and climate are the three major components that combine to make up this magnetic Life Energy. Magnetic land "holds" the "memories" of events, life-styles, and energies of the past, more so than any other type of terrain. Such countries also seem to be more oriented toward long-developing traditions than most others. In more electrical places, such as Egypt, the past is stored more in the actual man-made monuments rather than in the soil itself. Native American Sacred Sites in the Southwest are yet another example of this.

The countryside of England is beautiful and powerful. A short drive out of London in any direction provides the traveler with a tranquillity born from the greenest of green rolling hills, spectacular coasts, and the quiet of gentle pastoral settlements. One gets the feeling of being in the past and the present all at once and, as a result, finds a peace that is so often inherent in highly magnetic places. The body and mind can relax completely. I remember sitting in the lovely, tranquil gardens at the Chalice Well in Glastonbury on a warm summer day in June of 1986. The magnetism of that sacred place was quite seductive, and before long I found myself drifting slowly into a state of deep relaxation and peace. After a while the thought came to my mind that within the sanctity and safety of this place, it was hard to believe that in the world outside there could be war, death, hunger, loneliness, or any other of the ills and fears that plague mankind so cruelly.

King Arthur

A knowledge of England is incomplete and virtually impossible to pursue without encountering one of the most intriguing and enduring legends in history, that of Arthur, High King of Britain. The greatest figure in British folklore, Arthur lived during the late fifth and early sixth centuries at a time when the country was engaged in a bloody struggle to protect itself from the invading Saxon tribes and their allies, the Picts and the Scots. Arthur became the embodiment of hope for the people, uniting Britons and their land against their aggressive foes with the help of twenty-eight knights who comprised the legendary Knights of the Round Table.

Arthur grew up with both pagan and Christian values. Born from the "magical" arrangements of the Druid priest Merlin, which led to a coupling between Igraine, Duchess of Cornwall, and Uther Pendragon, Arthur came into life at a time of both political and spiritual change. Late fifth-century England was a country in transition, a time when the old pagan ways, though still flourishing, were being actively threatened. Eventually they gave way to the incoming new religion of Christianity. Arthur was sensitive to both because he was raised Christian, but tutored in pagan teachings by Merlin and the Lady of the Lake in Avalon. The hope for the future lay in his hands. His life became one of seeking peace and prosperity for the people. Interest in the tales that surround Arthur, his knights, and royal court have never waned, and they have much appeal today. Modern research has uncovered many answers that say that behind the legends of King Arthur, there was a real person of historical significance who lived in those troubled times. As we shall see, there are numerous Sacred Sites and power spots that have long been associated with Arthur the King.

The Living Past

An interesting twist to the history of the British Isles concerns a long lost civilization. England is not without its Atlantean legends. The western tip of Cornwall in the so-called Land's End district has some unique features that set it aside from the rest of the country and make it one of the most intriguing parts of Britain. The area consists of a high, bare granite plateau broken into by wooded ravines. Steep, picturesque cliffs border the sea on all sides except to the northeast, where it is connected by a narrow isthmus to the mainland. This small area contains the greatest collection of ancient monuments to be found anywhere in the British Isles or in the world. The collection is comprised of stone circles, menhirs, and dolmens, as well as Sacred Sites related to modern Christianity that were once the shrines of ancient Celtic saints. Some of these may date as far back as 6000 B.C.

It is believed that the Cornwall area was once much larger than it is now, for much of the long lost territory lies hidden beneath the sea. There is little doubt that this peninsula area has seen many successive inundations. It has also suffered gradual erosion, not counting any probable sudden geological catastrophes. This lost land, perhaps once a great kingdom, is called Lyonesse. It is believed that the Scilly Isles were once a part of Lyo-

nesse, just as some believe that the present Hawaiian Islands were once a part of the lost Lemuria. Legends,
artifacts, and actual sightings of underground remnants
of ancient Britain all point to the existence of a lost civilization that may very well have been a part of the huge
Atlantis. The area that is now undersea constitutes a
magnetic grid and may also be the site of any number of
natural vortices that, although no longer accessible to
man, continue to hold the powerful Life Energy charge
that sustains the Earth's body and consciousness for times
yet to come.

England's history has made its impact felt around the
world. It is truly an ancient empire whose global influence has rested in the areas of culture, intriguing personalities, battle, and its ever-growing society. The country's
landscape is one of the most celebrated in the world and
has been made memorable through countless paintings
and lyrics of artists down through time. There can be
little doubt that it is England's past that holds many precious secrets of our ancestry. These memories are held
in the substance of hundreds of standing stones and
megalithic sites, from Stonehenge to Avebury, making
the landscape read like the pages of a wonderful and exciting storybook. In traveling to these sacred places, the
pilgrim gets an opportunity to tap into the ancient past,
to refresh and renew the soul, and pay honor to the indwelling Earth spirit. Perhaps there is no other land in
the world that is more inhabited by the spirits of as many
profound human prototypes than Britain. In order to truly
appreciate what time has left for us in England, we must
gain some basic understanding of the people who left the
sacred landscape behind. Above all others, it is the Stone
Age people and the Celts who hold the key.

During the Stone Age, stone structures of varying types
were built all over Europe. Their meanings are still unknown, although theories, ranging from their being ceremonial sites to calendars that marked and linked Earth
with the heavens, have been presented. It is also believed
by many researchers that an ancient people constructed
the stone masterpieces upon land areas that possessed

particular and unusual properties. These natural energies were not only recognized but also played an important role in the daily and spiritual lives of the people. In the words of author and megalithic expert John Mitchell, "It was a form of magical technology. The power of the ancient shrines was augmented by the erection of stone monuments or temples, where the local spirit was induced to dwell and follow human example and become domesticated." Could it be that the Ancients' knowledge of these natural Earth energies and their association with them bestowed some sort of magical powers that we have lost sight of and, therefore, belief in? Did they tap into a knowledge that gave them an awareness of, and a subsequent use of, mathematics that would have otherwise been far beyond their intellectual reach? Were these a sophisticated people and not simple farmers or savages? Was theirs an ordered and well-governed society? I believe so. The real question then becomes: Can we learn what *they* knew? Can we tap into their memory by going to the great stone monuments they left behind? To this inquiry I must also say: I believe so.

The Celts came to Britain about 600 B.C. In terms of their calendar, government, and priesthood, it's likely that they assumed the ways of those before them. They knew of the stars. They honored specific gods and goddesses who embodied various forces of Nature. They believed in immortality, perhaps in reincarnation, as did most peoples who were astute observers of the natural Law of Cycles. Their religion was one of honoring and working with Nature and was not at all unlike that of the Native Americans of the North American continent. Their priests, the Druids, had special powers. They worked, consciously, with the power of the stars, the Earth, and the inhabitants of the realm of spirits.

Sacred Sites

As stated earlier, England, in its entirety, is a large magnetic grid. In order to identify the major vortices and

Sacred Sites there, I have chosen to divide the country
into three main regions: The Southwest, the North Country, and the East Country. I will point out each site according to the proper region, beginning in the Southwest,
the location of the shires (counties) of Devon, Cornwall,
and Somerset. Within these boundaries lie some of the
most sacred of England's land. This area of the country
is easily accessible from the north and the midlands on
the M6 (motorway) and M5, from London on the M4 to
M5. A more direct connection can be made from London
on the A30. However, the road is older and therefore
slower.

The Southwest

This area of England includes the shires of Wiltshire,
Dorset, Somerset, Devon, and Cornwall.

Dozmary Pool: This is the magnetic vortex from which
the fairy arm produced King Arthur's magical sword, Ex-
calibur. It is located in Cornwall on Bodmin Moor northeast of the Hurlers stone circle.

Woodhenge: Although none of the original markers
remain, this circle is marked with wooden markers instead of the more common stone ones. The configuration
of this circle is similar to Stonehenge. It is located north
of Amesbury on the A345.

Saint Michael's Mount: At one time this holy hill was
joined to the mainland, as evidenced by the remains of a
forest that have been found under the sea around it. The
mount is off the coast at Penzance on the A394 in Cornwall, and it is the location of a powerful magnetic vortex.
The vortex's energy is at its strongest at high tide. This
is an excellent site for a vision quest and to seek "visions" of angels. It is here that luminous images of the
archangel Michael have been seen.

Another distinguishing feature of Saint Michael's
Mount is that it is the beginning, or ending, depending
on one's perspective, of the famous Saint Michael's ley
line. This invisible Earth current extends through south-

western England to Land's End in Cornwall. Authorities consider the ley line to correspond to the legendary path that Christ took on his journey from Cornwall to Glastonbury. It is also a pilgrimage route for ancient travelers that is still used by many today. There are several Sacred Sites and vortices along the ley, which I will point out as they are mentioned.

Avebury: This small village is located five miles west of the town of Marlborough in Wiltshire. Take the A4 to the A361. Avebury is the largest stone circle in Europe. True to the systems of Feng Shui and geomancy, every stream, hill, and ditch holds symbolic significance in this area. I personally find the energy of Avebury, a strong magnetic vortex, extremely peaceful and relaxing. During my last visit there in the fall of 1988, I kept getting psychic impressions of the ancient people who had once inhabited the area. I sensed that they were of slight stature and quite nature-oriented. I also felt that they erected the massive stone circles for ceremonial usage, possibly to activate and generate the Earth energies there to a finely tuned peak of power to be used, in turn, for honoring the goddess, and for healing and the insurance of strong fertility powers for both the land and the people. Some believe that the design of the circles goes together to form a serpent. If so, not only is it reminiscent of the serpent mound areas in Ohio, but it would also indicate a specific ceremonial time.

Avebury is at about the center of the Saint Michael's ley system. Nearby are long barrows believed to have been used for burial, avenues, and earth ditches and enclosures. The mysterious, and largest, man-made earth mound in Europe, Silbury Hill, is there as well.

Silbury Hill: This artificial mound is the tallest prehistoric structure in Europe. The monument stands just beside the road A4, fifteen hundred yards south of the village of Avebury at the junction of the A4 and the A361. Silbury Hill is 520 feet in diameter, round in plan, and surrounded by a ditch from which the mound's material was dug. It is thought to be a round barrow, constructed during the Bronze Age by the same people who built the

Avebury henge. No conclusive date or purpose has been given for Silbury Hill. It is known to be pre-Roman and is thought to have been either the burial site of a king or high-level member of the ancient society who built this intriguing mound. However, there are also those who think that it may have been a ceremonial site alone. Until further excavations occur, Silbury Hill will remain one of the world's most mysterious man-made monuments. Albion says it is a unique man-made beacon vortex. It is also a magnetic vortex.

Stonehenge: In Wiltshire, eight miles north of Salisbury on the A303, are the most famous megalithic ruins in the world, Stonehenge. After seeing other stone circles, one realizes that Stonehenge is unique. The silent gray stone giants, sometimes called the Giant's Ring, stand on the Salisbury Plain, in clear sight from miles around. Earthworks, burial mounds, and other ancient monuments litter the general area, telling the Seeker that this was truly a special place. It still is.

It is believed that the henge was constructed over four thousand years ago. Some think it is even older. Built in stages, the circles are composed of stones, varying from the rough local sarsen of the so-called heelstone to Welsh "bluestone" and green sandstone.

There is little doubt of the calendrical purposes that Stonehenge served. The alignment of the axis with midsummer sunrise in one direction and midwinter sunset in the other constitutes the one feature of the site upon which all agree. Most believe it to have been a sun and moon temple, as both are evident in the particular alignments decoded in the middle 1960s by American astronomer Gerald Hawkins.

An integral part of the Stonehenge enigma concerns not only what the stone circle was used for, but who built it and how. Theories range from the builders having been ancient giants, to the Druids. Theories of the methods used in construction also vary, from the levitation of the stones by no less than Merlin himself to their having been floated to the present site on barges on the Avon River and then dragged by pulleys and set up. Still the mystery evades us, and if the truth be known, the answer probably lies somewhere in the middle, between the fantastic and the practical!

Stonehenge is a powerful magnetic vortex whose energy can be felt long before the monument is actually in view. Its vibrations speak clearly of being in the presence of an arcane Cosmic Temple. The ceremonies that must have taken place there! In John Mitchell's book *Sacred England*, he writes: "A temple in the ancient world was designed for invoking the particular god or gods to whom it was dedicated." He further writes: "The learned priests who built Stonehenge were concerned above all with keeping the lives of their people in tune with the seasons and rhythms of nature."

I agree, and I also feel that being in the aura of this powerful megalithic energy can help individuals attune to the inward recesses of themselves, to be better able to identify how and why they may be out of balance with Nature so that they might recenter by utilizing the Stonehenge power. It can facilitate balancing and harmonizing our subtle bodies and consciousness. I know I have come away from this sacred place feeling far more balanced and refreshed, and that I had gained back my power.

During a visit to England in the summer of 1988, as I lay on the sacred ground surrounding Stonehenge, Albion imparted some very interesting thoughts to me regarding the history of the area and the people who inhabited it. I made my attunement through Albion, and the stones of Stonehenge sang of an ancient, pre-Celtic race of Tall Ones, gentle giants who inhabited the sacred area on the Salisbury Plain. Here is part of what I experienced:

The stones began to vibrate and sing. . . . A procession of a hundred or more Tall Ones, dressed in animal hides, carry an Old One, a great elderly giant, on a lift made of tree trunks with a seat adorned with green boughs. His eyes are closed. I know that he cannot open them until he is put down, placed in the entryway to the Great Circle. Torches adorn the entire processional avenue. They smell of burning fat and hide. Black smoke pours from them, and waves of visible heat.

There are a few women standing at the entryway awaiting the arrival of The Elder. They are the Keepers of The Great Womb they called BA'KA'. The Great Womb is represented by a circle burned into their garments, as well as by the great stone circle itself. I know that as The Elder enters the stone circle, he will be, symbolically, reentering the womb. Once he is in place, he will be spoken to by the gods regarding the coming year. This ceremony is the Grand Rite of the year, a time of prophecy and revelation from the gods to The Elder. It culminates in sacred intercourse between the firstborn male and female of the two tribes (clans) represented. The female has been smeared with some sort of white paint or dust. She is naked. The male is also naked, with a circle painted on his chest. The women greeting The Elder are past participants in the Grand Rite ceremony—priestesses of The Elder.

It is lingering daylight . . . dusk . . . and the ceremonial fires grow brighter as the light gradually disappears. I know that the ceremony will go on until first dawn, when the prophecies will be given and spoken by The Elder. His name is . . . HAN. There has already been a sacrifice of a large animal, an auroch. The blood was kept, dried, and used for blessings, as well as a kind of spice for future meals. Each family was given a share.

This rite was held at a special time of the year, perhaps summer solstice. The Elder "read" the future twelve months, according to the particular configuration of stars overhead at the time. It was one of the few times in the year that the sacred spoken language was used. The rest of the time, a sign language was used. They believed that the sounds of the sacred verbal language went to the ears of the Great Ones (gods), whereas silent language (signing) was heard only by mortals.

When the prophecies were spoken, the helpers prepared the tribal calendar sticks, to be marked as "day" counters. The Elder blessed them. A sacred hide was carried into the stone circle and marked according to the predictions for special days (eclipses, comets, rain, flood, drought, etc.).

The Elder carried a great calendar stick made from a branch approximately twelve feet long. All the days of the people's existence were marked on this special ceremonial pole. The Elder wore aurochs antlers on his head at ceremonial times.

Another ceremonial time was Childbirth Time, the Birthing Ceremony. Physical sexual intercourse was engaged in during one moon phase (approximately twenty-eight to thirty days) each year. Intercourse was *only* for reproduction. Abstinence was the way of life all through the rest of the year. This was strictly obeyed, for a child born out of ceremonial sanctity would have been considered a child born from BA'AL and would have unleashed untold evil upon the people. Surely such a child and its unholy parents would have been put to death.

During the Birthing Ceremony, the women and the midwives were led into the stone circle, where they stayed until they had given birth. Any deformity or stillborn was blessed, and the dead were buried right away. The handicapped were given over to the Caretakers to be raised along with the "normal" children. A deformed child was considered a "special one," whose life of challenge set an example of the triumph of overcoming physical hardship. It was believed that from time to time these special souls were sent to live among the people as a reminder of the capability of the human spirit. How different it is for us who are "civilized"! The Birthing Ceremony took place over one lunar phase until all the births were complete. The Old Priestess (oldest of the Priestesses of the Grand Rite) would bless the newborns, and a feast was held, and then the children were taken by the Caretakers for rearing. This was a celebration, a true occasion of joy. It also freed the women for tending to their men, cooking, and other daily tasks.

The last of the three annual ceremonies involved a celebration of death. The Death Ritual was not a negative or sad occasion, but a solemn one, and it took place in the winter. At the time of death (no matter when it occurred during the year), the deceased were wrapped in animal hides after the flesh had been seared off their bones. They were wrapped very tightly, with the skeleton in a loose fetal position. The so-called Wrapped Ones were put into a pit that had been dug. White chalk dust was wiped on the outside and inside of the wrap hide. If it was a man, a piece of antler was placed inside, along with a few prized tools of his daily work. If it was a woman, the baby teeth of her little ones were placed inside. The more teeth she had with her, the greater her spiritual status.

At the time of the Burial, a great feast was held. Afterward, the Wrapped Ones were brought by procession into the stone circle to The Elder for special blessing. They were allowed to lie in state (inside the inner circle) for one lunar phase. Then they were removed and buried in catacomblike subterranean burial pits, stacked according to family.

This was not a highly populated people. Their average life span would have been about twenty to twenty-five years. The Elder was over fifty, thus his status. The Death Ceremony was called the "NO FIRE RITUAL."

Of all the megalithic sites in England, Stonehenge is the most heralded . . . protected . . . loved. None other strikes a greater chord of wonder in the *minds* of people. Perhaps if it struck a chord in the *hearts* of man, there would be no ropes here, no need to protect this treasure from man's willingness to play and tamper with his own ancestral inheritance.

Old Sarum: Located two miles north of Salisbury, in Wiltshire, is the prehistoric military and religious center. It is a man-made vortex and, as with almost all such artificial vortices in England, is electromagnetic. Also, this famous earthwork lies on a major ley line conjunction that is magnetic. It is believed that the new city of Salisbury succeeded Old Sarum, which now lies in ruins. The site can be reached on the A345 road and is open daily.

Salisbury Cathedral: A Sacred Site, man-made, very magnetic and situated on the same major ley line as Old

Sarum, this is lauded as one of the most magnificent cathedrals in England. It was built between 1220 and 1266, and the 404-foot spire can be seen for miles around. The cathedral is open daily, and there are guided tours. This is a wonderful spot to go for prayer. It is located in Salisbury.

Saint Catherine's Hill Chapel: This is but one of the many places in the British Isles where one can get in touch with the strong, ever-present female goddess energy. The chapel is situated on top of a conical mound which, at one time, may have been the site of ancient processions and ceremonies. This is another pagan site claimed by Christianity, as is so often the case in England. This is a beacon magnetic natural vortex. This location is easily accessible and is near Abbotsbury, nine miles southwest of Dorchester on road B3157.

The Cerne Giant: Located eight miles north of Dorchester on A352 is the famous chalk figure of a male giant! The figure has been carved into the terrain by unknown prehistoric artists, and its presence forms one of the few electric vortices in Britain. Solar energy is very strong here, and it may be because it was once the site of a solar temple or earthwork.

Glastonbury: Known long ago as Ynis Witrin, the Glassy Isle, Glastonbury in Somerset is the location of the famed Isle of Avalon. No other town in England has as many claims to its fame than Glastonbury, and from so many perspectives. One can come to the heart of Avalon from Christianity, through the legends of Joseph of Arimethea, who was the uncle of Jesus, the Arthurian legends, the Holy Grail, Celtic myth, the Druids, or through English history itself.

Glastonbury lies in the center of a plain that was once an island, bounded on the north by the Mendip Hills and on the south by the Polden Hills. It is located outside of Bath on the A361. At one time the island was roughly circular and consisted of three hills, with a fourth, known as Wearyall Hill, which formed a limb out to the west. The island no longer exists, but the land is drained and fertile, with the town of Glastonbury covering the western half of the ancient isle.

Glastonbury is a totally magnetic grid and is populated with several natural and some man-made vortices. Dominating the landscape is the Glastonbury Tor, a natural hill that has been man-terraced. Most believe that the Tor gets its shape from a combination of "geological, agricultural, and religious activities." Author, teacher, and longtime resident of Glastonbury Nicholas Mann has shared his thoughts about the Tor with me on numerous occasions. In his booklet entitled *Glastonbury Tor*, he writes, "The Tor is a conical hill 518 feet high, with a one thousand feet long, whale-backed ridge sloping away to the southwest. It is covered in grass, apart from a small area on the southeast flank where erosion has exposed the underlying soil and rock." Atop the hill stands the tower remnants of Saint Michael's Church, destroyed by an earthquake in 1275. Mann has also revealed the presence of a sacred spring he calls the White Spring, which once flowed differently from now. "It now rises at the bottom of Well House Lane, just above the reservoir it once filled."

The Tor was and still is a place of pilgrimage. Every week hundreds of people climb the green hill to stand on its summit, which provides an astonishing view of the town and countryside below.

Popularized by Marion Zimmer Bradley's book, *The Mists of Avalon*, the Tor and vicinity are believed by many to have been the dwelling site of the famed Lady of the Lake of Avalon, priestess of the gods and goddesses of the ancient Celts. It is also thought that the Tor was once a ceremonial site of the Druids, as well as a place where sacred rituals were once performed in honor of Cerridwen, goddess of wisdom, prophecy, and magic. The Tor, a magnetic vortex, is open and easily accessible.

Chalice Well: Located at the foot of Chalice Hill, itself a magnetic vortex, is the sacred Chalice Well. The well derives its name from its long being associated with the Holy Grail. Many believe it to be the actual location where the Holy Cup, brought to Glastonbury after the crucifixion by Joseph of Arimethea, uncle of Jesus, was hidden. The well is fed by an underground river and puts forth twenty-five thousand gallons of water daily, no matter what climatic conditions prevail. Because of a high content of iron in the water, which turns the stones of the well chamber and flowing troughs red, it has also been called the "blood spring." Miraculous healing powers have long been attributed to the well. The garden now built around the well is particularly lovely and peaceful, a perfect place to be healed on all levels of body and consciousness.

The Chalice Hill and the Tor hill are pointed out by geomantic experts to embody male (Tor) and female (Chalice Hill) forces and forms in the landscape. Such is reminiscent of Feng Shui.

On a trip to England in the summer of 1988, I spent an entire morning sitting in the garden, writing, allowing myself to be healed by the energy of this holy place. I asked, mentally, to speak to the Spirit of the Holy Well. It was early morning and there was a misty chill in the air. All around me was green, dotted with multicolored flowers. The Spirit began to speak through my hand. I wrote:

Every little green sprout is precious. To grow, that is the true meaning of life. Every one individual plant is just as individual as you. If you could hear the moans and groans of life coursing through the roots and stems, through every leaf and bough, you would know how utterly alive the whole world truly is. These green ones grow in silence. They make no spectacle of growth . . . only quietly do they respond to life.

The presence of the sacred waters causes humanity, when they come here, to come in a peaceful way . . . rarely showing any negative humanness that results in pain and grief. All harmonizes here. Where there is harmony, there is love. Where there is love, there is growth.

Blood spring, bringing forth from the body of Mother Earth the strength of iron . . . giving strength to the blood of man's body. When the blood is strong, the heart is strong. But when the blood is weak, limbs and life fade and die. There must be blood for Earth to live, for man to live. They are no different.

As I sat in the sacred garden that morning, I became acutely aware of the seemingly automatic and profound effect Sacred Sites have on mankind. Sacred places are places at peace. They seem to be protected from the world. Harm does not enter here. It cannot survive. All can be at peace and at rest here. I watched people as they came to the holy waters of the well. One young woman, alone, pulled out a small pewter chalice. First she washed her face and hands in the sacred water, and then splashed it on her hair. She touched a drop to her heart, brow, throat, and solar plexus. Then she filled the chalice and drank. Peace came over her face. Others came, one by one. Some washed their hands and face, all drank of the healing nectar. A man with a staff stopped at the well, looked, and left. An elderly couple came together and drank, several times. The woman with the chalice came again, sat down by the well, and began to play sweet melodies on a flute.

A place of pilgrimage sees so many personal ceremonies, not private, just personal, and done without shame. As I watched the responses to the water, I could not help but wish that everyone could realize that *all* water is sacred and treat it accordingly.

The Chalice Well is open daily, and a small fee is asked.

The Glastonbury Zodiac: In 1929 a young woman, an artist, made what she and many others believe to be an astounding discovery. While looking out over the landscape from atop a Glastonbury hill toward Cadbury, the woman became visually aware of gigantic figures outlined on the Earth. The outlines were marked by streams, roads, contour lines, and other boundaries, and formed, in perfectly correct positions, the map of the twelve zodiacal constellations! Katherine Maltwood's explanation of her discovery, as described in a book by Mary Caine entitled *The Glastonbury Zodiac*, is that the designs were natural to the Earth but refined by prehistoric residents of the area thousands of years ago. Tours of the Glastonbury Zodiac are available during the summer months.

Glastonbury Abbey: Located in the center of the town of Glastonbury are the ruins of the once magnificent Glastonbury Abbey. The ruins hint at the beauty this great structure once was, prior to its destruction during the reign of, and by, King Henry VIII. This place is reputed to have been the "greatest religious house in England." It has long been a place of pilgrimage due to its being considered the first Christian church in the world. The first church was said to have been erected out of wattle and wood by Joseph of Arimethea. The precious relic upon which the church was founded was believed to be the Holy Grail, the sacred chalice used at the Last Supper. The abbey also once housed the holy relics of Saint Patrick, an abbott of Glastonbury. The abbey is also said to be the location of the grave of King Arthur and his queen, Guinevere, based on the discovery of a gravesite in 1190 A.D. Tipped off by a bard, King Henry II passed the information to the Abbot who, a few years later, instructed the monks to excavate the site. Seven feet down, they found a stone slab under which was a lead cross that was etched with the inscription that translates to mean "Here lies buried the renowed King Arthur in the Isle of Avalon." The bones, of a man and a blond woman, were removed from the coffin that was discovered another nine feet below the stone slab, and were placed in a black marble tomb where they remained until the destruction of the abbey during the reign of Henry VIII. It is not known what happened to the bones during the resulting rifling and vandalism on the grounds. Today, a sign marks the spot where the grave was found. Few believe that the bones were truly those of King Arthur and his queen. The lead cross has also disappeared.

The abbey should be studied prior to a visit in order to fully appreciate the long and complex history of this remarkable and magnetic Sacred Site. The ruins are open daily, and it is a wonderful place for meditation.

Camelot: Located eleven miles southeast of Glastonbury off the A303 is the village of Cadbury, which is the site of the famed castle of King Arthur, Camelot. A ring of four large earthworks surrounds the top of the hill, and ancient wells, including the so-called Arthur's Well, are located around it. The archaeological excavations completed in the 1960s, at what is known on the maps as Cadbury Castle, seem to concur with the legends of Arthur and his time. Although it is a steep climb, the hill fort is open to the public. The wells, Arthur's and Saint Anne's, are on the site and easily found. This hill is a natural magnetic vortex.

Wookey Hole: Located two miles northwest of the town of Wells, the Wookey Hole is a cavern with a subterranean river. This is a natural magnetic vortex site and was once believed to have been used for ceremony. A modest admission fee is charged.

Stanton Drew Stone Circles: Located about twelve miles north of Wells on the B3130 road are a series of stone circles believed to have been the site of a Druid Mystery School. There is a modest entrance fee charged.

There are many more Sacred Sites in the area of the southwestern region that are too numerous to mention. However, those listed here are the major ones. Others may be discovered by travel in the area.

In the peninsula area of Cornwall and Devon, there are several sacred wells. Each is a natural magnetic vortex. There are also several prehistoric monuments in the general area.

Saint Cleer's Well: Saint Cleer is located two miles north of Liskeard near Bodmin Moor. The well is clearly marked near the center of the village. The water is said to cure blindness and lunacy.

The Hurlers: Located two miles north of Saint Cleer on Bodmin Moor, it is believed to be a site of prehistoric rituals.

The Cheesewring: This Neolithic rock pile is on the summit of Stowe's Hill, one mile north of the Hurlers. It is also linked with the Druids, as well as a possible astronomical marker. It is marked, but it is a hike off the road to the monument.

Tintagel: Allegedly the birthplace of King Arthur, the ruins of Tintagel Castle are located in the town of the same name. Tours are available from March through October daily. Take the A39 from Camelford, the B3266 to Boscastle, then the B3263 to Tintagel.

Merlin's Cave: On the beach just below the Tintagel Castle ruins is a beautiful cave associated with Merlin, the Magician. The cave is easily reached and may be entered at low tide. This is a powerfully magnetic area and a wonderful place for quiet time.

Merry Maidens Stone Circle: Located on road B3315 at Boleigh, the Merry Maidens stone circle is the site of several megalithic monuments, barrows, stone circles, and holed stones. These may constitute an ancient ceremonial site, and they emit a strong energy current.

The North Country

The North Country includes the shires of Cumbria, Northumberland, Durham, and York.

Castle Rigg Circle: Located near Keswick on the River Greta, Castle Rigg is believed to be an ancient Druid site. Because of the surrounding landscape, this is an electromagnetic vortex. The circle is open, and there is no admission.

Long Meg and Her Daughters: This is the largest stone circle in northern England. Located twenty miles northeast of Penrith in Cumbria, this area was definitely ceremonial and astronomical in purpose.

Lindisfarne: Known as the Holy Island, Lindisfarne is situated off the Northumberland coast in the northeast corner of England on an island that is approximately three miles long. The ruins of a castle and priory have long been a site of Christian pilgrimage and are easily accessible at low tide.

Robin Hood's Well: Located near the Fountains Abbey ruins, a Christian sacred site, this well is associated with

Robin Hood and his band of Merry Men. The well is on the left bank of the River Skell.

Mother Shipton's Cave: This site is associated with the famous prophet and gifted seer Mother Shipton, and is said to be her birthplace. It is a highly magnetic area and is also the site of the infamous "petrifying" well that is said to turn objects to stone.

The East Country

Shrine of the Virgin Mary: A strong magnetic vortex, this active pilgrimage center is located in Little Walsingham, forty-six miles east of Ely. There are several other sacred places in Little Walsingham, many active pilgrimage sites.

Healing Well: The well is a monument to Saint Withburga. It is said to have remarkable healing powers and is located in the cemetery of the church of Saint Nicholas in East Dereham.

Cathedrals and churches are certainly Sacred Sites, as many of them were built over ancient pagan ceremonial and/or vortex sites and areas. The following is a list of some of the major cathedrals and churches and their general locations throughout England. These are wonderful sites for prayer and meditation.

Westminster Abbey—London
Saint Paul's Cathedral—London
Saint Alban's Abbey—Hertfordshire
Winchester Cathedral—Winchester
Canterbury Cathedral—Canterbury
Salisbury Cathedral—Salisbury
Wells Cathedral—Wells
Exeter Cathedral—Exeter
The Church on Saint Michael's Mount—Penzance
Gloucester Cathedral—Gloucester
Saint Ethelbert's Cathedral—Hereford
Chester Cathedral—Chester (Welsh border)

Carlisle Cathedral—Carlisle
Durham Cathedral—Durham
York Minster—Yorkshire
Fountains Abbey—Yorkshire
Rievaulx Abbey—Yorkshire
Byland Abbey—Yorkshire
Jervaulx Abbey—Yorkshire
Mount Grace Priory—Yorkshire
Ripon Cathedral—Ripon
Lincoln Cathedral—Lincolnshire
Ely Cathedral—Ely
Peterborough Cathedral—Peterborough
Old Churches of Fenland—Fenland

CHAPTER EIGHT

INDIA:
Land of the Sacred,
Nature, and Man

"Let your eye go to the sun;
your life to the wind . . . go to heaven, and
then to earth again."

HINDU PRAYER

Indian History and Geography

India, the seventh largest country in the world, is a
land filled with people. A poor nation, India is constantly
having to deal with the ever-present, ever-expanding
problem of overpopulation that results in a lack in virtually every aspect of human life and society. In spite of
its difficulties, however, the country still functions as the
Earth's largest democracy.

In many ways, India can be called a "land of contradictions," some of them social, others economic. Still,
India survives, challenged by the caste system, multiple
languages and the separations that result, and poor income, which has threatened to divide and destroy for
centuries. As with Tibetans, the only one true unifying
factor is religion. Hinduism is the faith of over 80 percent of the country's population, with about 60 percent
of those being orthodox in their persuasion.

INDIA

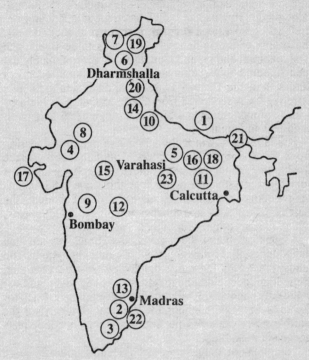

1. Mount Everest
2. Swamimalai
3. Palani Temple
4. Mount Abu
5. Allahabad
6. Darmshalla
7. Amarnath Cave
8. Lake Pushkar
9. Ajanta
10. Almora
11. Bodh Gaya
12. Ellora

13. Kanchipuram
14. Hardwar
15. Ujjain
16. Varanasi
17. Dwarka
18. Deer Park
19. Kulu Valley
20. Rishikesh
21. Darjeeling
22. Auroville
23. Khajuro

The country's vast mainland is comprised, basically, of three well-defined regions. These include the mountains of the Himalayas, which stretch some fifteen hundred miles west to east, forming a crescent-shaped wall, the basins of the Indian subcontinent's three rivers, the Brahmaputra, Indus, and Ganges, also approximately fifteen hundred miles long and some two hundred miles across, and the Deccan Plateau. A peninsula area, this third region is separated from the Indo-Gangetic Plain by a mass of mountains and hills that range up to four thousand feet in height.

The Himalayas are truly a rich and beautiful blessing from the Creator. The highest mountain range in the world, the Himalayas are home to over ten peaks that soar to twenty-five thousand feet above the land and its people. Among them is the majestic Mount Everest, the Earth's tallest peak and most powerful electrical vortex, which is shared by India, Tibet, and Nepal.

Aside from being the highest, the Himalayas are also the youngest and longest east-west mountain system. The landscape within the range includes snow-clad summits, sprawling ice fields, huge glaciers, deep river gorges, waterfalls, and wide valleys, each providing a feast for the eyes and nourishment for the soul. Other than the Earth's poles, there is no area on the planet that rests under snow and ice.

The plains of India cover almost half a million square miles, constituting a huge natural electric grid. It is this area that is the most highly cultivated due to the availability of water. The plateaus, the oldest part of the country's land surface, consist largely of ancient crystalline rocks in varying stages of deformative change that has taken place over the last five hundred million years. India has almost every possible type of soil, ranging from the alluvial, which is composed of mud, gravel, and sand that has been deposited by water, to arid, mountain, hill, black and red, and swampy lowlands. This would indicate the presence of electric, magnetic, and electromagnetic Life Energies in the terrain. The country's climate is determined by rain-bearing tropical monsoons that result in four complete seasons. However, annual rainfall and temperatures vary widely.

As one might think, India has a wide variety of both vegetation and animal life. Animal life includes some of the world's "big game" species, such as the tiger, panther, cheetah, elephant, bear, deer, antelope, and gazelle. Two species of wolves populate the region, as do the jackal, lynx, wild dog and pig, and the buffalo. Although the infamous cobra is the best-known of India's reptiles, there are others, some poisonous and some not. Approximately two hundred species of birds share space with domestic animals that include mules, camels, horses and ponies, cattle, sheep, and goats.

Indian Philosophy and Religion

However, India is her people. Her present-day inhabitants are mostly the product of many past invasions that have swept the country, resulting in much intermingling. This has given rise to Caucasian, Mongoloid, Negroid, and Australoid, each contributing to the language variations due to population movement.

People naturally seek spiritual expression. Therefore, one of India's distinguishing human features is that it is the birthplace of many religions. Hinduism, Jainism, Buddhism, and Sikhism are the chief religions, while others, such as Christianity, Judaism, and Islam, have been growing as extraneous groups. Of these, Hinduism is India's truly traditional faith. Its origins date back to between 2000 and 1500 B.C. It can certainly be said that Hinduism is a unifying force. But its association with the caste system, which is a rigid, hereditary social class system based on wealth, birth, and rank, has made for a dividing separateness.

Indian philosophy both differs from and agrees with western thought on the nature of Reality. If we asked the question, does knowledge arise from experience or from reason, the western mind analyzes; the eastern mind intuits. Basic Indian philosophy is composed of a wide diversity of views, theories, and systems, making it virtually impossible to detect characteristics that are shared by all its people. The Vedic hymns, which are sacred Hindu scriptures that date from the second millennium B.C., are the most ancient records that tell of the process by which the human mind makes its gods and goddesses, as well as the deep psychological significances involved that lead one to the most profound cosmological concepts and truths. In addition, the Upanishads, which are philosophical treatises, contain one of the first conceptions of a universal, all-pervading spiritual Reality that leads to an essential unity of matter and spirit. These treatises also contain the Indians' views of Nature, life, mind, and body, along with addressing matters of ethics and social philosophy.

Actually, three specific basic concepts form the foundation of Indian philosophy: *atman*, the self or soul; *karma*, actions; and *moksa*, salvation. These concepts and their interrelations form the manner in which the people live and think.

Karma is the most typically Indian of the three. Karma signifies the moral efficacy of human actions. The idea of "reaping what one sows," although not totally absent in western thought, results in a far more profound operation of the Law of Cycles in eastern religion, that being *reincarnation*. While the belief in reincarnation is growing in the West, it is still primarily an eastern concept of truth.

The *atman*, also not altogether absent from western ideology, is the belief in a transcendental or Absolute Self. This is similar to what westerners have referred to as the soul.

Moksa embodies the "highest ideal" that humanity can reach, both individually and collectively. Christianity has indeed addressed such an issue, but from different perspectives and perhaps, on an individual pursuit, with a lesser degree of diligence than the Hindus.

A unique feature of Indian thought and its development is its systemization of each into what is called *sutras*, which means "threads." Each sutra is a concise expression of a doctrine that reduces elaborate philosophies into memorizable formulas or rules. The sutra literature began prior to the rise of Buddhism in India, whose similar sutras have a much different style, somewhat like sermons, that carry the thread of the Buddha's teachings. Some of the earlier sutras, known as the Kalpasutras, are not philosophical, but ritualistic. These deal with sacrifices, ideals, prohibitions, and morality.

We cannot truly acquire an understanding of India and its people without understanding the reigning religion. Hinduism is both a conglomerate of religions and a civilization. There is not a definitive beginning to it all, nor a founder, nor a central authority figure, nor an organizational hierarchy. Therefore, any concrete definition of Hinduism is not complete or satisfactory. However, we can approach this ancient faith with certain knowledge that is central to its power. The belief in a Sole Reality that is the Ultimate Cause and Source and is the goal of all existence must be the beginning point of understanding. The Hindus call this Ultimate Reality *Brahman*. Brahman *causes* the universe. Brahman transforms itself into the universe and assumes its appearance. Brahman is in all things. Brahman is the Creator. Brahman is the reabsorber of all things. Brahman, indeed, is the sole central focus of India's spiritual life.

An Indian's contract with the unseen or sacred is through rituals that are designed for the purpose of sustaining the universe of which man is an indissoluble part. Cosmic processes make earthly life and well-being possible. These processes, it is believed, are governed by order and truth, an order and truth that must be protected from destruction by chaos.

Hindu gods and goddesses preside over certain parts of the Cosmos and/or are responsible for both cosmic and social phenomena. Not all such deities are anthropomorphized, but all embody powers, both the personal and impersonal inherent in Nature and man.

The temple is the focal point of human worship. The divine words carved on the temple doors serve to remind the faithful of the need for change before a human can truly enter into the realm of God. Festivals, which are complex combinations of religious ceremonies, involve eating, lovemaking, feeding the poor, music, and dancing to renew the people and help them surmount critical obstacles and generate power. Such refreshes the human soul. Likewise, pilgrimages to Sacred Sites also play an important role in helping the Hindu obtain purification, spiritual renewal, and freedom.

Within the many denominations of Hinduism, there are individuals who are inclined to abandon all material attachments and seek a life of devotion by joining an order or circle. Once the commitment has been made, the initiate submits to the rites and the way of life involved. Those considered qualified to initiate others are usually called the Brahmans, or gurus, who have themselves previously been initiated.

Iconography is a tremendous force in the Hindu religion. The beauty of the sacred objects invites divine powers into them, and they, in turn, express the supernatural. An example may be seen in the statue of the god Vishnu, second member of the Hindu Trinity of Vishnu, Brahma, and Shiva, who has eight arms. Four of the arms represent the four cardinal directions, while the other four illustrate the four-four concept of God: strength, knowledge, potency, and lordship. Indian spiritual art, which is also highly symbolic, is designed to represent an invisible idea. Artists must do more than create an object. They must place themselves into an altered state of consciousness in order to undergo a spiritual transformation that allows them to make the image a receptacle of divine power.

Because of the central role that religion plays in India, it is a land filled with Sacred Sites. It is also a land that is generously sprinkled with natural Earth vortices that are composed of all three Life Energies. In speaking to people who have traveled to India, one gets the feeling that, on the surface, it is a country buzzing with more noise, activity, fragrances, and feelings than one can imagine. In the book *A Pilgrim's Guide to Planet Earth*, it is said that "the passion of life is naked for all to feel, not covered up as Western sensibility demands. Most travelers either plunge blindly into this gushing river of life (often to be engulfed by it) or remain as separate and aloof as possible." Many people I have talked with speak of having experienced extreme "cultural shock" upon their arrival and during their stay in India. The lack of sanitation, dead animals, sometimes dead people, poverty, and disease can be quite unsettling. *The Pilgrim's Guide* says: "For those of us whose faith is newborn and feeble, India is an excellent place to work on developing faith and devotion. Wherever you turn in India, you are surrounded by fellow devotees."

Sacred Sites

Pilgrimage to India has its rewards, to say the least. In the land where ancient practices of spiritual responsibility are still followed, one can journey and participate in the pilgrim's dharma of giving food and alms at the sacred places. To feel and experience India's Sacred Sites, her people, and the land itself can be the ultimate of journeys with spiritual intent.

In general, the land in India is electrical in nature, and therefore inspiring, regenerating, and capable of awakening the soul into life and conscious action. As with all the countries considered in this book, the Sacred Sites and Earth vortices are too numerous to mention in totality. However, through the help of research, travelers to the area, and my own knowledge, I have compiled a list of the most notable of such sites. Whenever appropriate, I have also made comments as to the Life Energy charge of the vortex and/or grid locations.

The greatest source of magnetism is water. To the Indian, the River Ganges, like the Nile to the Egyptians, is the Mother. "The Mother nourishes and cleanses." Again, in the *Pilgrim's Guide to Planet Earth*, it is expressed so beautifully. "Ganga Ma Cal, the water which flows out of the top of Lord Shiva's head, is the manifestation of this energy flow." This sacred river is one of the major sources of pure magnetic life force in India, and constitutes, along with the Brahmaputra and Indus, the supply of magnetism to the land and its people. Likewise, the Ganges is a magnetic grid and the place of annual pilgrimage for cleansing.

Called by the local people Chomolungma, whose name translates to mean Goddess Mother of the Earth, Mount Everest is the highest mountain in the world, soaring 29,028 feet into the skies on the India-Nepal border. This awesome peak is not only sacred, but it is also the most potent electrical vortex on Earth. The peak, which Albion has called "a point of light," is the watchtower, with its watchful eye upon the location of two lands that contain within their national and racial consciousness the most ancient of all religious thought forms. A tremendous amount of sheer power is continually emitted as an electrical force that sustains life and spreads prana all over the globe.

Temples

India is a land of temples. Each is a unique and special place of learning and worship. Perhaps one of the most desirable temple pilgrimages is to the southern peninsula of India, where there are six temples, each of which holds special reverence to the people. Each of these sacred temples is representative of man's chakras:

Tirupara Kunram: A location that is considered the holy mountain of the Lord. It is an electrical vortex.

Trichendur: A magnetic vortex of healing energies.

Swamimalai: Also a magnetic vortex area. It is called "the Heart of the Universe."

Palani Temple: A magnetic vortex known as a spiritual oasis.

Tututani: An electrical vortex. This means "Lord of the Mountains." "Nowhere else on Earth provides a more powerful inspiration to do good than this temple" was Albion's comment.

Alakar Malai: An electromagnetic vortex, which represents the "Third Eye" in man.

Bodh Gaya: This is, perhaps, one of the most special electrical vortices in India. It marks the spot where Buddha attained enlightenment. Spending time here can achieve the same for the pilgrim.

Amaranth Cave: Located in Kashmir, this is an electromagnetic grid. It is sixteen thousand feet high, and this contributes to the makeup of its energies. When reached, it is an excellent spot for healing and meditation.

Mount Abu: Located in the Rajasthani Desert, this is the site of the Jain temples. This is an electrical grid area. Mount Abu is a major Jain pilgrimage site.

Allahabad: Three sacred rivers, the Ganges, the Jumna, and the Saraswati, meet here. It is a magnetic vortex area that facilitates cleansing and inner healing.

Darmshalla: An electrical vortex where the attuned person can hear the "music of the spheres." This is the current home of the Dalai Lama from Tibet. Although its energy is electrical, its power can transform such force into purely magnetic energy. It transforms aspiration into receptivity. This is a good current through which the Dalai Lama can send his thoughts out to the world.

Lake Pushkar: A magnetic vortex and a sacred Godlake. Its water is capable of carrying one's consciousness into a highly receptive state. It is said that Lake Pushkar was created when Lord Brahma dropped nectar. Every November full moon, people come to the lake to take a dip in the sacred waters.

Ajanta: This is a magnetic grid located in western India. Caves with ancient rock drawings are here, holding much of the land's memory.

Almora: Located in the foothills of the Himalayas, it is seven thousand feet high in some places. This is the home of the guru Govinda. It is most interesting to note that above this area, atmospherically, there is a break in the Van Allen belt, a region of space that has many highly charged and rapidly moving particles all trapped in its magnetic field. This makes Almora a highly charged electrical-magnetic location.

Bindu Sagar: Considered a sacred lake, Bindu Sagar is located in Bhubaneswar, the Cathedral City of India. It is said to have once had seven thousand temples around its shores, and now has five hundred. This is a popular pilgrimage site.

Ellora: Located thirty kilometers from Aurangaband are some of the most magnificent caves on Earth. The mountains here have been cut into sanctuaries, and there are thirty-four caves. One of the caves is dedicated to Shiva and is most likely the largest monolithic structure in the world.

Girnar: Located near Junagaah, this is the second most sacred hill to the Jains, second only to *Palitana*. There are five sacred Jain hills in India, and each is a natural electromagnetic vortex.

Amba Mata Peak and *Kalka's Peak*: Both are sacred areas and are small electrical vortices.

Seven Holy Cities

Kanchipuram: The site of many Dravidian temples and one of the Seven Holy Cities of India.

Hardwar: Seventeen miles south of Rishikesh, it is the "Doorway to God."

Ujjain: A Hindu holy city.

Varanasi: Called Benares, it is the ancient abode of Shiva.

Mathura: It is the birthplace of Lord Krishna and a Hindu pilgrimage site by the Jumna River.

Ayodhya: This is the birthplace of Lord Rama, and the site of many temples.

Dwarka: This is the Holy City of the West, sacred to Lord Krishna, and is one of the four main Hindu pilgrimage sites.

Modhera: This is the site of a sun temple.

Ragjir: Here Buddha spent nine years and Jesus three years. This is an electromagnetic vortex and the site of a hot radioactive mineral spring. This is a healing and peace center.

Sankasya: It is here that the Lord Buddha descended to Earth, and it is the location of the ruins of many monasteries and ancient monuments.

Deer Park: Located outside Varanasi, it is the place that is also called Sarnath. It marks the birth of Buddhism because it is the site where the Buddha gave his first sermon and set into motion the Wheel of Dharma—the "law (s)" or disciplines and principles of Buddhism. It is also often referred to as the Wheel of Life.

Sravasti: This is an electromagnetic vortex and was the site of the Buddha's greatest miracle. This site can trigger deep-seated intuitive powers. It is now a wilderness area called Saheth-Maheth.

Arunchala Mountain: This is the abode of Shiva, one of the most highly charged places in India. Circling the mountain is a pilgrimage, and it is said to take from three to twenty-four hours. It is also the site of one of the largest Shiva temples in India. This is a purifying electrical area.

Sikkim: A strong magnetic grid area. Here one can attune to the Mind of God. The highest peak here is Mount Kanchenjunga, a twenty-eight-thousand-foot peak whose name means "the Great Snow of Five Treasures." This is a strongly colorful and intensely active electrical vortex.

Razir and *Kulu Valley*: These are both highly magnetic due to the presence of powerful healing springs. Both Jesus and Buddha are said to have come here. The Kulu Valley is magnetic and a spot where angelic beings congregate.

Rishikesh: A magnetic grid that, due to the constant use of its energies, has coagulated into a full-blown magnetic vortex. This place can trigger latent psychic powers, especially for the purpose of "seeing" into the future. Latent healing powers can also awaken here.

Darjeeling: In the writings of Alice Bailey, based on information given from her "source" known simply as The Tibetan, this is one of the five sacred cities of the world where Life Energy is transported through a major ley system between here and London, Tokyo, Geneva, and New York. The use of the term ley line is my own but fits well with what Bailey states about the "connection" between these cities and the similarities of their energies.

Punjab: Ram Dass's healing center.

RAM DASS: An American who, particularly during the 60's and 70's, became a very famous "guru," teaching ways to self-awareness, taking responsibility for self, and meditation and other ways to enlightenment. Ram Dass was Richard Alpert Ph.D. who, after getting into LSD (and other drugs) experienced a transformation. He went to India and learned yoga and meditation techniques which he teaches in the West.

Anantapur: Sai Baba's home.

SAI BABA: Sai Baba is a world-renown guru (East Indian) who is known for his ability to manifest objects out of the blue (I don't know how to say this any differently). Many westerners are followers of Sai Baba, perhaps more than any other guru in the East. He has never been to the United States to teach. His ashram is in Anantapur.

Auroville: Aurobindo's home.

AUROBINDO: Aurobindo was an East Indian Yoga Master, born in August of 1872. He lived for fourteen years of his life in the West and then returned to India and entered into his spiritual work. He returned to India when he was 20 years old.

Punjab, Anantapur, and Auroville are three man-made vortices that Albion has pointed out. Each has potent healing and empowering electromagnetic energies.

Khajuro: Site of the Brahman and the Jain temples, which are both highly magnetic spots that are conducive to the healing and revitalization of sexual energies.

Albion's concept of the Earth having chakra centers not unlike those in the human etheric body is, as far as I know, a unique teaching. If we turn to and rely upon C. W. Leadbeater's teachings regarding the Sanskrit word *chakra*, we find that "the special use of the word chakra with which we are at the moment concerned is its application to a series of wheel-like vortices which exist in the surface of the etheric double of man.'' These vortices take in energy from our environment, process it, and put it back out. The Brow Center or chakra, which Leadbeater calls the ''sixth centre,'' is located in a human between the eyebrows. This is the center that gives us *insight*.

When we relate this concept to the Earth, we can get a glimpse of the possible way the land and its energy have contributed to the nature of the people and their spiritual practices and beliefs. India and Tibet form the Crown Chakra of the Earth, with the energy in Tibet being the most potent. Other planetary chakras are located in the Ring of Fire in the Pacific Ocean, the Kundalini Center; the so-called Four Corners region of the American Southwest, the Heart Center; the center of the Gobi Desert, the Crown Chakra; the mid-Atlantic, the Earth's Solar Plexus; Alaska, the Spleen Center; and the island of Puerto Rico, the Throat Chakra.

India is open to all travelers. It is also said that the Indian gurus are open to receiving Seekers who are interested in personal spiritual growth, even without prior notice. Bringing an offering to the Sacred Sites and the natural Earth temples is something I always encourage. A gift of food or flowers is also a good idea in the event the visitor gains audience with a spiritual teacher.

Whenever you go and wherever your travels in any of these countries may take you, go with peace in your heart. Give back to the Earth of your own powers. Do not just ''take'' of the Earth's energies.

In the beautiful writing entitled *The Blue Planet*, by Louise B. Young, the author states: ''We who inhabit the planet Earth are still far from knowing the Truth about our home in space, but every day we come closer to an understanding of the world of phenomena. The leaves of the lotus are unfolding. In recent years we have discovered many strange facts. We have totally revised our view of change and becoming.'' When I asked Harley Swiftdeer for his view of the present conditions on our planet, he replied that he ''sees'' several things. ''Yes, people have been and are coming around. But by the time people have come awake, it is almost too late. There is so much damage. Because of this, the Great Spirit must use chaos as the tool of correction . . . hurricanes, fires, death . . . and many two-leggeds will go down . . . others will be passed by. We need more and more ceremony to repair the damage done to Mother Earth. I am trying to help survival through the Twisted Hair teachings.'' Swiftdeer explained these teachings as going beyond the Native Traditionalists, beyond the dogma of the tribes. ''The Twisted Hairs entwine many teachings and philosophies into a working, living knowledge for today. I must take the medicine out to wake up all the people. We must come to realize that we are all Earth people. Only through ignorance man gives his freedom away. We must restore the Earth back to beauty.''

Indeed we must! It is hoped that, as we continue to seek to reconnect ourselves once again to our planetary ''mother,'' we will experience many more ''changes'' and ''becomings.'' Our individual and collective pilgrimages to the holy sites on the sacred body of the Earth can uplift and inspire us to good. The awakened latent faculties within us that result can serve to guide us toward a greater and better life and future. It can insure us that there will indeed be a future for ourselves and our blue planet. Although this book is designed, primarily, to point out the many Sacred Sites man has built on the Earth's body, we would do well to keep in mind one very important fact, that being that the whole Earth is sacred. The entire planetary form is a ''living Life Temple,'' ever-growing, changing, and evolving toward the Light of Understanding. That process of evolution is not the Earth's nor ours alone or separate. We are one. We are one. We are one.

You now have a good idea of where on Mother Earth many of the Sacred Sites are located, and perhaps you are already planning a pilgrimage. In the following chapter you will learn how to specifically connect with, experience, and use the Life Energy System.

PART III

CEREMONY:
THE DANCE
OF LIFE

CHAPTER NINE

CEREMONY:
Embracing the Power
of Mother Earth

We believe the land and the people are one. We believe that only people with an integral relationship to the land can survive.

GEORGE BARTA, Sioux

The Art of Ceremony

The art and practice of ceremony are sorely lacking in the daily lives of most people today. Perhaps one of the major causes of this lack can be placed at the feet of religion, whose priests and clergy perform staunch traditional rituals while the faithful are mere onlookers. And perhaps our modern, high-tech society and fast-paced life-styles leave us little time or *inclination* for individual spiritual practice. There may also be an even more basic truth which lies in modern man's ''disconnection'' with Nature, a disconnection that has resulted in our thinking that we have no *need* for interacting in a ceremonial way, or any other way, with the forces and energies inherent in Nature or within other life-forms with whom we share the planet Earth. The need for spiritual nourishment on a purely personal and individual level fades when it goes so long without satisfaction. We tend to push such needs aside, perhaps, until the emptiness left by them dies out and we no longer recognize, consciously, what is truly missing or what we have lost.

When we look back over the ages of human history, we find that, to our ancestors, ceremony was a way of life. It was a part of life that was designed to recognize and honor the "spirits" and "forces" that they sensed and who were given credit for their lives and its happenings, both good and bad. Our current obsession with progress, especially in the West, does not leave much room for such practices as daily ceremony. We pride ourselves in what we have "outgrown." We do ceremonies only on special occasions.

Although the wheels of change roll slowly, this omission of ceremony from our daily lives, and the subsequent spiritual malnourishment twentieth-century man suffers from, could be changing. One by one we may be awakening to the truth that balance involves both our outer mind and body and our inner being or soul. Both of these aspects of ourselves must work together in order for a state of equilibrium to exist and to yield the desired result of self-confidence, courage, good concentration, positive direction, and a well-balanced ego/personality. The realm of the sacred can be entered even when we are devoid of such psychic equilibrium. But we cannot "see" when we are in such a state, and we cannot gain true insight that we can bring into the everyday world to serve as practical tools for the elevation of consciousness and personal conscious evolution.

Basically, ceremony serves three important human needs. First, it is an excellent tool for our "reconnection" with the complex forces and energies in Nature. In this capacity, the ceremony becomes a personal cosmic drama enacted by the individual who seeks communion with certain "powers." The motives and forces contacted may vary. The ultimate conclusion of the experience is usually similar, most often it is one of fulfillment, or at the very least, satisfaction from attempting the alignment itself. I have participated in private personal ceremonies and have led many group ones over the years.

It is rare for me to feel "let down" after such an event/ experience. I have witnessed the same response of uplift- ment and peace in others.

Second, ceremony is a purely conscious act. Whether or not the operation consists of words and actions that are traditional and, therefore, prechoreographed for us, or our rite is self-styled, it does not matter. That is one of the wonderful things about doing a ceremony. We can let our movements, words, and offerings be from our hearts. However, I do not suggest that we change existing traditional ceremonies that have been taught by the native people of any culture, for I believe we should honor as sacred the rites that have been handed down for centu- ries. When we are fortunate enough to have firsthand knowledge of such ceremonies, we can, by doing them as they have been done for so long, connect ourselves with, and participate in the ancient "thought form" that has been generated by the minds and hearts of many gen- erations. Such thought forms are very powerful and can do much to link us to the energies and spirits that reside in the Sacred Site we may be visiting.

When no such traditional ceremonies are known or we are incapable for some reason of practicing them prop- erly, then we may create our own rites to suit the site and/or occasion we wish to honor. Whichever the situa- tion might be, there are certain preparations, both inward and outward, that should be achieved. Going through these preliminaries also gives one the opportunity to think and plan even more thoroughly for the ceremonial event. The following is a step-by-step checklist for helping to insure proper preparation. You may utilize these steps as you see fit, and add to them any further ideas that would help to insure the best possible results.

Ceremonial Etiquette in Ten Easy Steps

STEP 1: Grounding. Before entering the sacred area: Sit on the Earth. This serves to connect you to the Earth, to *ground* you, if you will. Take a few moments to relax the body and still the mind, in order to put yourself into a state of openness. When you feel that you are in the proper frame of mind, there can be a "receptiveness" to the energies of the Sacred Site. In this state of openness, the flow of your own energies is an offering in itself, and they can move outward to the Sacred Site more freely. Those energies may be directed to the site for the purpose of a general Earth healing, or specifically for healing the particular power spot. It may also be transmitted as pure love energy.

STEP 2: Smudging. "Smudge" before entering the sacred area. Smudging is a common ceremony for cleansing the aura and body of any negative thought forms and energies, and it is used by Native Americans. The usual herbs and/or plants used for smudging are: *sage*, for general cleansing (Any variety of wild sage will work fine); *sweet grass*, for attracting good spirit forces and positive energies; and *tobacco*, for additional cleansing. Pure tobacco may be obtained from most specialty smoke shops.

The smudge herbs and plants should be thoroughly dry for good burning. You may wish to gather and prepare (drying and mixing) your own smudge. Otherwise, the proper plants or smudge sticks may be purchased from various suppliers or New Age shops. A proper vessel for igniting the plant substances will be needed, along with a fan or, perhaps, a feather for keeping the heat going once it has been lit. The smudge "bowl" may be a large shell such as abalone, a piece of pottery, or a box turtle shell.

When the herbs have been placed into the smudging bowl or object, they should be ignited. When the fire lights the mixture, it may be fanned, gently, until it is smoking nicely. Next, place the bowl on the ground. Kneeling down, cup the hands in the smoke and pull it over the face. Then, cupping the hands once again, pull the smoke over the head. Repeat the process until the cleansing smoke has been spread over the entire body. The remaining smolder may be used to cleanse any ceremonial objects you may be using.

STEP 3: The giving of your offering: When the offering is something physical, it should be chosen carefully. If your gift is nonphysical, such as a chant or song, a mantra, a dance, or some other form of prayer, it should be made at the appropriate time, silently if there are others present, or aloud if you are alone. If you are a part of a group, one may be selected who will lead the group in a particular meditation or ceremonial procedure, which you can follow accordingly. As I mentioned at the end of Chapter 3, offerings may be herbs, such as sage or tobacco, or one that has a special significance to you. Or you can use a few of your hairs, a small crystal or other mineral, or something that just "feels right" to you. Remember that the offering will be left behind, so it shouldn't be something that will deface the site.

STEP 4: Water Offerings. If you have come to a particular Sacred Site, such as a holy well, for healing, it is acceptable to drink the water or to take of the healing waters in a gentle manner. I feel good about bringing a water offering to such places and simply pouring it on the ground nearby. This is symbolic of giving back to the healing waters so that they might be forever replenished. Such an offering is also a gift to the "water spirits" of the place whose essence is the power of life and transformation. When taking water from a sacred well or spring, be frugal. Some sites sell water containers for a minimal cost.

STEP 5: Honoring. If you visit a Sacred Site that you know has been used for specific ceremonies in the past, then it is good for you to honor that use. This may be accomplished in one of three ways:

• By performing the exact same ritual/ceremony that has been performed there in the past.

• By doing a ceremony that you have designed that is in keeping with the purpose for which the area has been used.

• By quieting the mind and body and opening yourself to the energies of the place, visualizing the ancient rites that have taken place there. I have known such a meditation to reveal sights and sounds of past sacred rites.

This is a good way to open to the "ancient voices" of the environment, both physical and nonphysical.

STEP 6: Dreaming. For several nights prior to your ceremony, pay attention to your dreams. They can be quite revealing and may also contribute to your ceremony by showing you specific or related images and insight. Also, dreams can be a good source of guidance for telling you that a particular ceremony may not be appropriate for you. They may also reveal past life connections you may have with a given Sacred Site, ancient cultures, and/ or certain ceremonies.

STEP 7: Prayer. When it is time to leave, leave in peace. I always leave by offering a prayer. Prayer suggestions for benediction include:

• Prayer for the blessing of the spirits and energy forces of the Sacred Site.
• Prayer for Earth healing.
• Prayer for world peace.
• Prayer for you to live peacefully and that you might walk in better balance on the Earth.
• Prayer for your enlightenment for the sake of all that lives.
• A blessing prayer for all lives on Earth.

STEP 8: Special Ceremonies. There may be occasions when you are invited to participate in a special ceremony that is going to take place at the Sacred Site you are visiting. Examples of such an event include the Sun Dance, a Sweat Lodge, a pipe ceremony, or a medicine wheel ritual. During these times the medicine person or shaman will lead the procedures, and you should simply follow by executing your own role in a proper manner. In this way, your knowledge and your inner and outer awareness will be increased.

STEP 9: Listening to Guidance. If you are visiting a Sacred Site and you feel unqualified to do a ceremony or uncomfortable because what you have chosen to do is not in keeping with the purpose of a particular site, then it in keeping with the purpose of a particular site, then it is a good idea to honor those feelings. They may be quite intuitive and not due to any sense of self-lack. Only you can determine your own particular feelings and sensitivities at a time like this. There have been many occasions when, for days prior to my visiting a power spot, I have received psychic impressions of things that would be appropriate for me to do while I am at the site. My advice is to always follow such inclinations. At the time of the visit to the special area, there is just as much to be gained by simply sitting quietly and observing Nature's splendor. This is a wonderful opportunity to renew your personal relationship with Nature and her powerful creative forces. It is an equally valid time for allowing the high energies of the place to inspire you, and to give you thoughts that may serve as guidance to you on your daily life path.

STEP 10: Giving the Self. No matter what the personal motives and circumstances may be that have led you to any given power spot, remember to leave something of yourself behind. Uniting with the residing forces and spirits is accomplished by your offering(s), ceremony, meditation, and/or prayer. As you leave the site, you might visualize a stream of pure light flowing forth from your heart to the Earth and the environment of the sacred place. This is a simple and effective way to give some of your power to the site. As I said earlier, you may also wish to leave a hair from your head as a symbol and offering from yourself.

Ceremony As Transformation

While performing your ceremony, you may become aware of intense energy patterns and/or spirit forces and entities, for ceremony truly is the "moving" or "stirring" of such energies. These energies and your interaction with them is *magic*. Channeling or directing these powerful energies, along with your own, is necessary in order to bring about personal transformation. This *is* the ultimate motive behind ritual: personal transformation.

Ceremony can result in a profound change in one's level
of consciousness and awareness. At other times, the
changes may be much more subtle. In any event, it is
best to be aware that your ceremony will *change* the balance of things, around you and within you. All the more
reason to realize that we must not bring about such
change without knowledge and without being fully aware
that it will serve some need.

It is certain that the use of ritual or ceremony comes
from and awakens the psyche deep within an individual.
It teaches us and helps us to tap sources of power that
are truly unlimited and infinite. It opens us to Nature's
powers. It is both a right- and a left-brain affair, for it
makes use of the physical and intellectual parts of our
mind consciousness, as well as the intuitive soul faculties.

Diet and Clothing for Ceremony

There are a few more helpful hints regarding ceremony
and your visit to Sacred Sites that I feel are important to
point out. The first of these involves diet. Some feel that
it is important to fast for several days prior to a ceremony. As a part of the inner cleansing and preparation,
this makes good sense. While I do not personally feel it
is necessary to engage in a prolonged fast, I do feel that
fasting for several hours prior to visiting a site is a sen-
sible practice. The length of the fast is really up to you.

There is also the matter of clothing. Some traditional
ceremonies require the participants to be adorned with
masks, headdresses, or special clothing. If you are involved with such an occasion, you should follow the instructions of the medicine person or leader of the event
as to what garments or other attire are necessary. When
you are performing a private ritual alone, it is best to
follow your own personal inclinations. Keep in mind that
while certain attire, such as a robe, can do much to help
you to get into the proper frame of mind, you do not
want to overdo. Perhaps the rule to follow would be that

clothing or adornments should not *attract* undue attention nor *distract* your attention from the matter at hand.

If you are making up your own ritual, then keep in mind that it is not necessary to use the same procedure each time. Allow room for spontaneity. Small changes are fine and can prevent you from falling into a habit or pattern of simply giving lip service to a rite and/or going through the motions without really thinking about them.

Working With Energy

Also, physical, emotional, and mental relaxation are very important to the success of any ceremony. Furthermore, the ability to work properly with energy also greatly depends on your personal sense of integrity, courage, and level of wholeness. None of these vital qualities can or should be taken for granted. Neither can they be automatically assumed to be present or taught to you by any other person or teacher. If one or more of these qualities is absent, or if a comfortable level of relaxation and confidence is not achieved, then the flow of energy may be blocked. Another possible result is that the flow of psychic current through you and/or from you will meet with a stressing resistance, causing a great deal of the power to simply be drained away. This will drain you, as well. Ceremony, naturally, expends a lot of energy. It takes energy to move energy around and to interact with Nature's powers.

In coming to truly understand ceremony, it is also important to recognize that *energy* is the level and force(s) that you are working with. So it is *energy* and its nature that one must come to know. Perhaps such an understanding begins in a workable definition of the term *energy* and then moves on to comprehending its implications. When we have these firmly established in our mind consciousness, I believe we have a better chance of dealing properly with energy in its varying forms and to know how it affects us on all levels of our lives.

The Holt Intermediate Dictionary of American English

defines energy as "the material power of the universe
. . . mental or physical force." *Power* is the key word
here. This definition implies that matter possesses an
"occult" or *hidden* nonphysical essence. That essence
empowers the universe, and gives it life in the form of
motion, which is known as kinetic energy. This movement animates the universe and all its forms. This motion, then, is an indication of *life*. By this definition,
energy becomes the living current or force within all
things.

Energy moves in a circular motion, in spirals. Viewed
in this manner, we see physical evidence of energy's behavior in various shapes in Nature. Whirlwinds, whirl-
pool galactic designs, the nautilus and other shell forms
and patterns, dust "devils," and the helix evidenced in
the all-important DNA molecule all witness energy's
fundamental course of activity. Even though the pattern
of the flow of Nature's power is easily seen in these
forms, we must remember that energy is present and operating in *all* forms and in *all* particles of matter. So we
must use our imagination, the "tool" of our intuitive
faculty, to be able to perceive the exact same patterns in
everything that exists, from the tiniest single atom to the
most complex of molecules, including the body of man.

Yet another facet of kinetic dynamics is what I believe
to be true about energy, generally, no matter what form
within which it resides. All waxes and wanes. For example, we see evidence of this fact in the purely physical
operation of the Solar System where we live. The sun has
a zenith position to the Earth, a position where its power
is strongest in its effects. The sun also has a nadir, during
which time its effects are at a minimum in a given hem-
isphere. The moon waxes toward its full stage and then
begins to wane.

We know that this truth has a more personal application. We all go through periods when our physical, emotional, mental, and even spiritual vitality is recognizably
at a high or low ebb. With the birth of human psychol-
ogy, we are also becoming more aware of the subconscious or unconscious energies that are operating within

us. Various methods, usually in the form of therapies, have arisen to help us recognize and tap into these subtle but powerful forces deep within ourselves. To successfully deal with this aspect of our innermost consciousness, we must open to the Being or Soul itself. Besides therapy, per se, ceremony becomes a viable tool to communicate with the soul, whether it be with our personal, individual soul or the soul within all else. In the words of the remarkable educator and author Joseph Campbell: "Rites, then, together with the mythologies that support them, constitute the second womb, the matrix of the postnatal gestation of the placental Homo Sapiens." In short, rites or ceremonies are the "roadway" by which we travel to the inner sanctum of all matter and Beings.

Waxing and Waning Energy

Waxing energy is energy at its fullest potential of power. During such times, energy, of any kind, positive or negative, has its greatest effect on matter. The interplay between form and energy at this time can be extremely intense, requiring careful and knowledgeable handling by those who seek to tap such power. Perhaps the most important thing one should keep in mind involves gaining an awareness of a proper *channel* for the force(s) in question. Ceremony is a way to channel energy. Other ways include the force being used to "trigger" and/or "awaken" one's intuitive faculties. This helps one to gain a deeper, more profound awareness, of self, of Nature and natural law, and of the quality of the energies themselves. Also, as one interacts, consciously, with the invisible subtle powers of Nature, one becomes more "connected" with those powers. This serves to "ground" and "center" one more perfectly in harmony with all life. However energy is channeled is a matter of personal choice that is, I hope, based on sound knowledge, judgment, and a deep degree of personal awareness.

Where and when energy is in a waning state its potency is at its lowest ebb or proceeding in that direction. During these times, one must put more conscious effort into any ceremony or other form of relating to the forces in question, because it helps compensate for the lower energy level.

Vortex Energy

Let us return, at this point, to the issue of performing a ceremony at a natural vortex or Sacred Site, keeping in mind that ceremony is the "manipulation" of energy. This is accomplished by several things that need careful consideration. We must remember to approach the area with respect. This cannot be stressed too many times. I once encountered a valuable statement made by an unknown person. It went: "You must not change one thing, one pebble, one grain of sand, until you know what good or evil will follow that act." I feel that the absolute truth of this statement is particularly useful in learning to better understand and deal with energy. This statement reminds us that we must be careful not to disturb the environment, any part of the environment, including that of an especially powerful or sacred place. It also points out to us that what may seem like the minutest and most insignificant of actions does indeed have an effect, one that could very well be far more profound in its repercussions than we expect. This is also true in reverse. The smallest of actions can have the most positive effects. Therefore, *all* actions must be conscious and well thought out.

Sacred Ceremony

Ceremony fulfills an inborn spiritual, even religious, need. This is the major, if not the only, reason that we have so-called Sacred Sites to begin with. Ancient man, with his special sensitivity to the Earth's energies and the places where its emanation was the strongest, performed his ceremonies over and over again in the same locations.

This generated an intense power that coupled with the natural environmental forces, resulting in vortices of great power that are still alive and can be felt today. While some Sacred Sites have been abandoned due to the fading and extinction of some cultures, others are still very much in use. Furthermore, I am of the opinion that many, if not *all*, of the sites are reawakening once again to full power at this critically important time of change on our planet. Evidence of this can be seen in the current appearance of numerous books and articles on the subject of Sacred Sites, the popularity of "pilgrimages" to honored places throughout the world, and the numbers of people who eagerly participate in such journeys and who seek out, personally, knowledge of high-powered places. This may have all been summed up by author Vine Deloria, who stated: "Unless the sacred places are discovered and used as religious places, there is no possibility of a nation ever coming to grips with the land itself. Without this basic relationship, national psychic stability is impossible." Such stability must begin with individuals before it can or will become a "national" force for good. Then it will spread to become a global stability. Deloria also says that what we gain from our individual experiences at a given place is "revelation." That revelation can be purely personal insight that will serve to help us aspire to and become a better person. It can also be the vehicle by which we can share what we learn with others, which can lead ultimately to the betterment of the planet.

In living our daily lives, we receive and give certain satisfaction, meet our challenges, succeed and fail. All is a part of being human. However, by engaging in ceremonial practices, we *receive* and *give* something, perhaps an *essence* that human power alone cannot give or receive. Ceremony gives renewal. It results, each time, in Transformation, in a sort of rebirth. Indeed, ceremony and ritual are tools of Transformation, and spiritually oriented rites are at the very foundation of culture and human civilization.

Let us now enter into a description of basic ceremonial

techniques. This format may be used as a guideline for ceremonies you wish to perform for any purpose. I will also give some suggestions on how this basic format may be refined and adapted to specific types of Sacred Sites and/or vortices, as well as for attuning to particular energies for giving honor and celebrating certain entities or natural energies.

To begin with, all ceremonies should take place within a circle, real or imaginary. You should not actually build a circle of stones, except when you are creating a ceremonial site on your own private land or using a circle or lodge that is already in existence at a given vortex or power spot. Otherwise, a mental circle is best. The "mind circle" is created by visualizing an intense orb of blue light. See it on the ground. Reinforce it for a few minutes or as long as it takes for its existence and perimeters to be firmly planted in your mind's eye. The circle may be as large as you wish. The center of the circle is the most powerful part. It is the place where energies merge and transformation occurs. Once the circle is firmly established, you may step inside to begin your ritual. If you have properly empowered your ceremonial orbit, you will know it once you enter its boundaries, for its energy is timeless, its power uplifting and at the same time incredibly peaceful. Its current is conducive to aiding your body and consciousness to reach the desired state of awareness and clarity. Each ceremony will require the building of the circle, and no rite should be conducted without one, for it also serves as a "psychic barrier" of protection.

First, go to the center of the circle and stand, or sit if you prefer. Be still. Allow yourself to become "merged" with the elements and forms in the environment. This is done through the breath. Breathe deeply, taking in the energy. As you exhale, know that your breath is becoming one with every tree and plant, the ground, the air, the rocks, the water, or any other life-forms present.

Once this "communion exercise" is completed, take your offering in hand and go to the Four Directions of the circle, always beginning in the east, then south, west, and north respectively. At each station, a bit of your offering should be given. If your offering is one object only, then place it in the center of the circle after the Four Directions have been honored. Honor is given by the utterance of a prayer and/or invocation for protection and harmony during your sacred rite. The Four Directions have been referred to and personified as, depending on the culture or teachings involved, the Four Spirit Keepers, the Four Watchtowers, the Four Archangels, and the Four Winds. This part of the basic ceremony fulfills our obligation to recognize and honor all the manifestations of energy. It acknowledges all as our "relatives."

Next, invoke the energy of the site to merge with you. This is best done by walking in a sunwise (clockwise) motion around the center of the circle, or around or within the Sacred Site itself, no less than seven times. As you do this, you should repeat a prayer, mantra, chant, or invocation designed by you to draw in the energy. Remember, energy moves in a circular motion. As you move, you will begin to "see" or sense the power increasing and expanding. Mentally, draw the energy into a spiraling "cone of pure power." Feel it elevate, feel it intensifying around you and within you. Allow yourself to be "caught up" in the center of the energy cone or vortex, merging totally with it. When the energy has reached its peak, stand or sit silently on the ground, within its force, breathing in the full power, allowing yourself to "float" freely in a high state of meditative receptiveness.

When the intensity of the energy and your experience with it has subsided, it is time to end your ritual. Silently go, once again, to each of the Four Directions. Give thanks and blessings to the spirit forces that have helped you. Return to the center of the circle. Draw in the blue energy of the circle you built by breathing it and absorbing it into your body and consciousness. Then leave the area in peace and in the love of the Creator.

Natural vortices and Sacred Sites have varying terrains. On occasion, the epicenter of the spot will have a specific form within which the energy is embodied. Such forms can include a sacred mountain, a holy spring or well, a stone circle or dolmen, a single stone monolith, a temple, a pyramid, or some other actual structure or shrine. There are even occasions when the object is a member of the plant or mineral kingdom. For example, the sacred tule tree in Oaxaca, Mexico, and the Kaaba, the sacred meteorite or black stone in the shrine at Mecca in the Mideast. When this is the case, your ceremony is best oriented to that specific object, whatever it may be. We should honor these forms as the vehicle *through* which we gain access to other dimensions of Reality.

In order to drop our egotistic and physical barriers and allow the power of the Earth to flow through us, ceremony helps to direct our thoughts, personal energies, and desires toward a higher, more refined state of awareness. In such a state, both the past and the future can open up to us, and we can truly soar beyond sight and explore hidden realities, for such energy states are timeless. This type of experience can be a very healing one. In fact, healing, generally, is perhaps the most sought after and desirable energy and experience we pursue.

A good, workable definition of "healing" is balance brought about after some level or part of ourselves has suffered damage. All too often we tend to take healing to apply only to a physical-level problem. Not so. The healing needed can be emotional or mental in its nature. Also, a need for spiritual health can be the most difficult imbalance to deal with. It can be a great source of insecurity to be confused or devoid of spiritual nourishment due to being off our chosen path for self-betterment or, worse still, not to have one at all. By reaching a high level and state of awareness, we are more likely to receive guidance that can help orient us to a spiritual path that is right for us. In short, when we are in such a state, we are more open and likely to listen to our inner soul voice, which can give the needed advice. Therefore, when we approach healing ritual or healing prayers, we must keep in mind that such is a petition for balance and harmony in our lives and bodies, or the lives and bodies of others. In order to avoid any karmic interference, I feel it is appropriate to simply ask for such a balance to occur. This can be achieved by *visualizing* health and contentment replacing the current adverse state of affairs. If you are asking for healing at a special site conducive to healing power, the sacred vortex should be honored. The following is a simple ceremony based on the format given earlier that may be used at such a site as a healing well, spring, or river, several of which you could encounter in the countries discussed in this book. It may be used, however, at any special water site.

To begin, go through your "centering" exercise and construct your ceremonial circle. Enter the circle and honor the Four Directions. Then proceed to the water source. Mentally address the spirit forces present and give your offering of water *to* the water in whatever manner is traditionally practiced at that particular location. If it is a spring or river, you may wish to submerge yourself. If it is a well or drinking spring, you may drink from it. Drinking from a special cup or chalice that is special to you helps to reinforce your receptivity. When you have finished, give thanks to the water spirit(s), honor the Four Directions, draw in your circle, and leave.

If you are visiting a sacred mountain, you have access to a huge reservoir of psychic power! Climbing to the summit, going partway up, or performing your ritual at a place at the base of the peak that feels "right" to you must be the first decision. Once you have decided upon the right spot, you may proceed by utilizing the basic ceremony I have given, unless you are participating in a group or some other prescribed rite. Energy from sacred mountains may be drawn up and used for any purpose you may wish. "Seeing" the cone of power you cogenerate with the mountain as encompassing the entire mount is a good way to focus the power.

When performing ceremony at a megalithic site such as a stone circle, medicine wheel, temple ruins, or other place that is or forms an "enclosure," you may enter into the area, unless regulations of the given site prohibit you from doing so. Always honor any such rules. They have been established for a good reason, usually to protect the area from vandalism. In such circumstances, you may do your ceremony as close to the site as possible. However, when you can enter the inner sanctum of such a place, you may follow the same basic ritual without constructing a mental circle enclosure. If it is a circular site, you may use the site itself rather than visualizing a circle.

Sun and Moon Ceremonies

Many Sacred Sites were built, specifically, in honor of the Sun and/or the Moon or by a culture of people to whom the Sun and/or Moon were sacred. There may also be occasions when the energy of a particular place is known to be most potent during a special solar day, time, or event, such as an eclipse, or at one of the quarters of the Moon, usually Full Moon. If you are present on these occasions, it is good to add a segment to your ritual that is designed to honor these celestial powers and spirits. It can fit nicely into a ritual done for any other reason. You may also choose to use these basic solar and lunar ceremonies at any place you may be when you feel the need to offer your respects to these bodies.

The Sun is pure "fire" power, the major source of electricity to the Earth and her life-forms. To give back, in thanksgiving, of our own energy is an ancient and traditional practice. Remember, unlike us, our ancestors took no natural phenomena for granted. To honor the solar force, you may simply face the Sun, give thanks silently or aloud, and then sprinkle cornmeal on the ground as your offering. Give thanks for its light, the life-giving power the Sun emits. Give thanks for the day(s) and the opportunity of living and growing that it brings.

In honoring the Moon, the same procedure may be used. Face the Moon and give thanks for the cycles of change she regulates within you, your life, and on the Earth. An offering of flowers, water, or fragrant incense or oils is an appropriate gift. When using these ceremonies as a part of some other ritual purpose, these simple instructions will suffice. However, when you are seeking to honor the Sun or Moon only, you will want to remember to honor the Four Directions. Always create your protective magical circle first.

If you want to honor the Moon, keep in mind that it is feminine and receptive, while the Sun is male energy and positive. At the time of the Full Moon, its energy is most potent. When it is in its waxing stages, the Moon's power is best recognized and used for the purposes of growth, productivity, and regeneration. During its "waning" process, it helps bring about endings and change. It also helps to destroy stagnation. When it is waning, its power is subsiding and it is best used to help you turn inward for self-searching, cleansing, and to assist you in harvesting the "seeds" you have planted.

The very heart of the matter of ceremony is *intent*. As long as we know, clearly, our personal motives, then we are likely to give to and receive from the energies of Mother Earth in the highest and best form. We will come to truly realize, not just intellectually, that the mind is a wondrous and magnificent "tool" for coming to the threshold of viewing life and its components and forms from the perspective of *wholeness*. Yes, appreciation of the beauty and life in Nature is to be thoroughly enjoyed. But when it is personally and individually experienced and expressed, we can then, and only then, understand and live within the power of greater soul enrichment.

Bibliography

Amon, Aline. *The Earth is Sore: Native Americans on Nature*. New York: Atheneum, 1981.

Batchelor, Stephen. *The Tibet Guide*. London: Wisdom Publications, 1987.

Bloom, William, and Marko Pogacnik. *Ley Lines and Ecology: An Introduction*. Glastonbury, England: Gothic Image, 1985.

Booz, Elizabeth B. *Tibet*. Lincolnwood, Ill.: Passport Books, 1986.

Bord, Janet and Colin. *The Secret Country: More Mysterious Britain*. London: Paladin Granada Publishing, 1978.

Briggs, John P., and F. David Peat. *Looking Glass Universe: The Emerging Science of Wholeness*. New York: Simon & Schuster, 1984.

Bryant, Page. *The Earth Changes Survival Handbook*. Santa Fe, N.M.: Sun Publishing Company, 1984.

Chaney, Earlyne. *Secrets from Mt. Shasta*. Anaheim, Calif.: Stockton Trade Press, Inc., 1953.

Fidler, J. Havelock. *Ley Lines: Their Nature and Properties, A Dowser's Investigation*. Wellingborough, Northamptonshire, England: Turnstone Press Limited, 1983.

Foster, Stephen, and Meredith Little. *The Book of the Vision Quest*. Spokane, WA.: Bear Tribe Publishing Company, 1986.

Freesoul, John Redtail. *Breath of the Invisible*. Wheaton, Ill.: The Theosophical Publishing House, 1986.

Goodman, Jeffrey. *American Genesis*. New York: Summit Books, 1981.

Hadingham, Evan. *Early Man and the Cosmos*. New York: Walker Publishing Co., Inc., 1984.

LaChapelle, Delores. *Earth Wisdom*. Silverton, Colo.: International College and Way of the Mountain Learning Center, 1978.

Lovelock, J. E. *Gaia: A New Look at Life on Earth*. New York: Oxford University Press, 1979.

McDonagh, Sean. *To Care for the Earth: A Call To a New Theology*. Santa Fe, N.M.: Bear and Company, 1985.

The New Encyclopaedia Britannica Macropaedia, vol. 13.

Pennick, Nigel. *The Ancient Science of Geomancy: Man in Harmony with the Earth*. London: Thames and Hudson, Ltd., 1979.

Schaefer, Vincent J., and John A. Day. *A Field Guide to the Atmosphere*. Boston: Houghton Mifflin, 1981.

Spence, Lewis. *British Fairy Origins: The Genesis and Development of Fairy Legends in British Tradition*. Northamptonshire, England: The Aquarian Press Limited, 1946.

Stone, Merlin. *Ancient Mirrors of Womanhood*. Boston: Beacon Press, 1984.

Watkins, Alfred. *The Old Straight Track*. London: Abacus Edition, Sphere Books Ltd., 1974.

Williamson, Ray A. *Living the Sky: The Cosmos of the American Indian*. Boston: Houghton Mifflin, 1984.

Wilson, Colin. *Mysteries*. New York: Perigee Books, 1978.

Young, Louise B. *The Blue Planet*. Boston: Little, Brown, 1983.

About the Author

Page Bryant is an internationally recognized teacher and lec-
turer in the fields of metaphysics and psychic phenomena. She
is the author of THE NEW EARTH CHANGES SURVIVAL
HANDBOOK and founder of the Mystic Mountain Teaching
and Retreat Center in Asheville, North Carolina. At the Center
she holds residential seminars and workshops on such topics
as astronomy, physics, astrology, psi-development and other
ancient wisdom traditions.

An expert in Native American mythology, Bryant has been a
long-time teacher at the Medicine Wheel Gatherings sponsored
by the Bear Tribe. She is also an outspoken advocate for Friends
of the Earth, Greenpeace, and the Cousteau Society.

Those wishing to contact the author can write to her care of
the publisher at:

> Ballantine Books
> 201 E. 50th St.
> New York, NY 10022